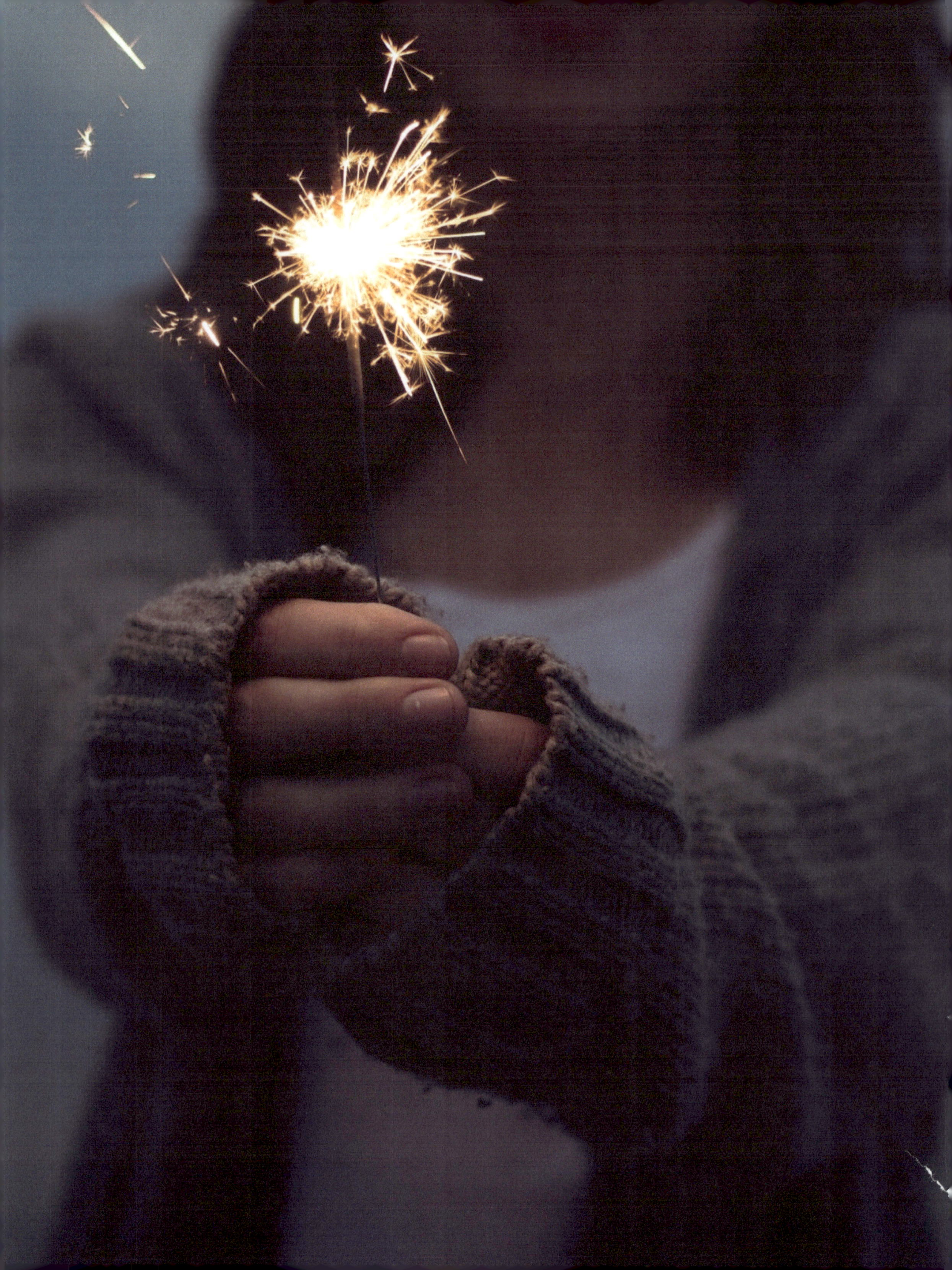

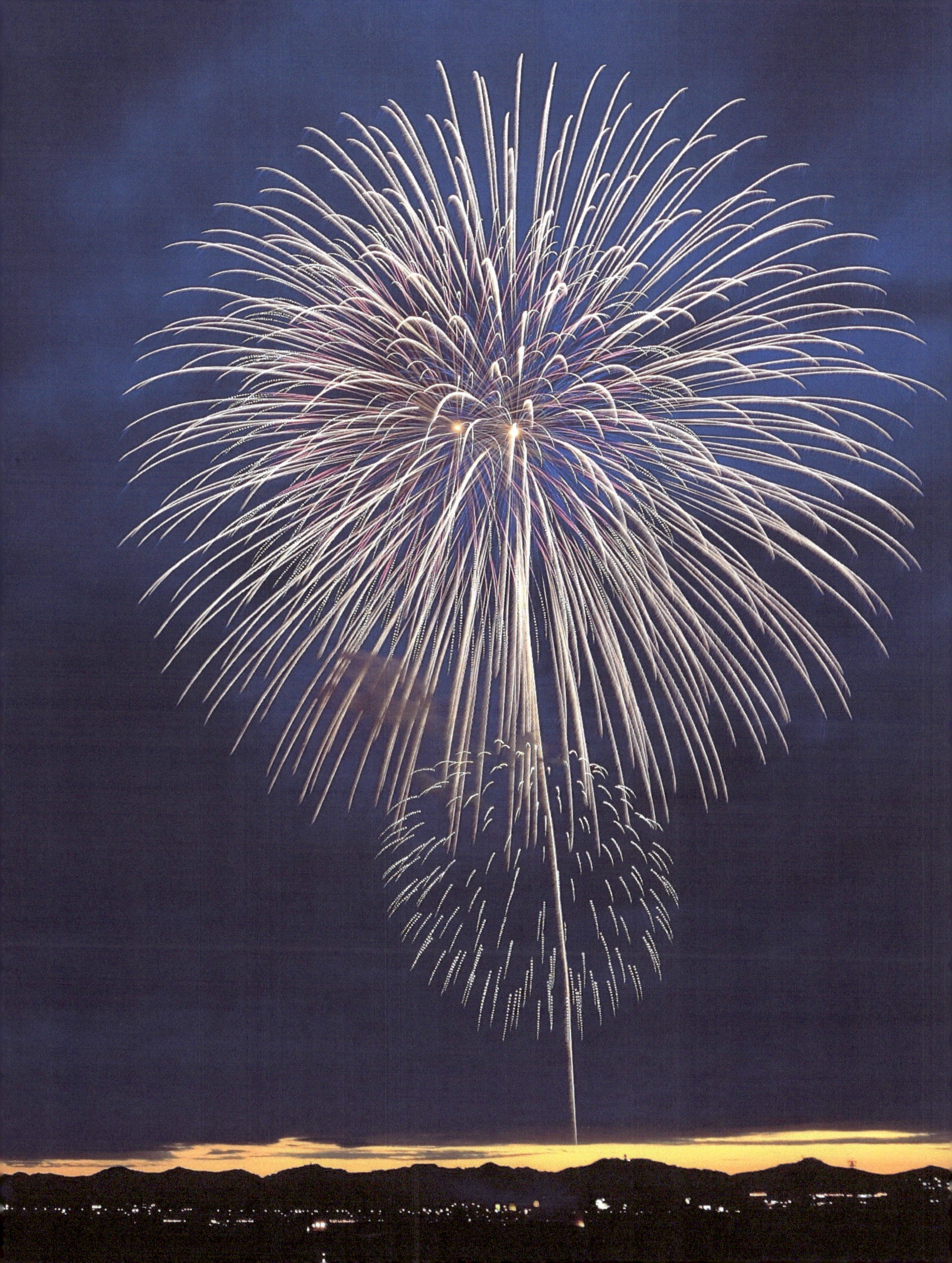

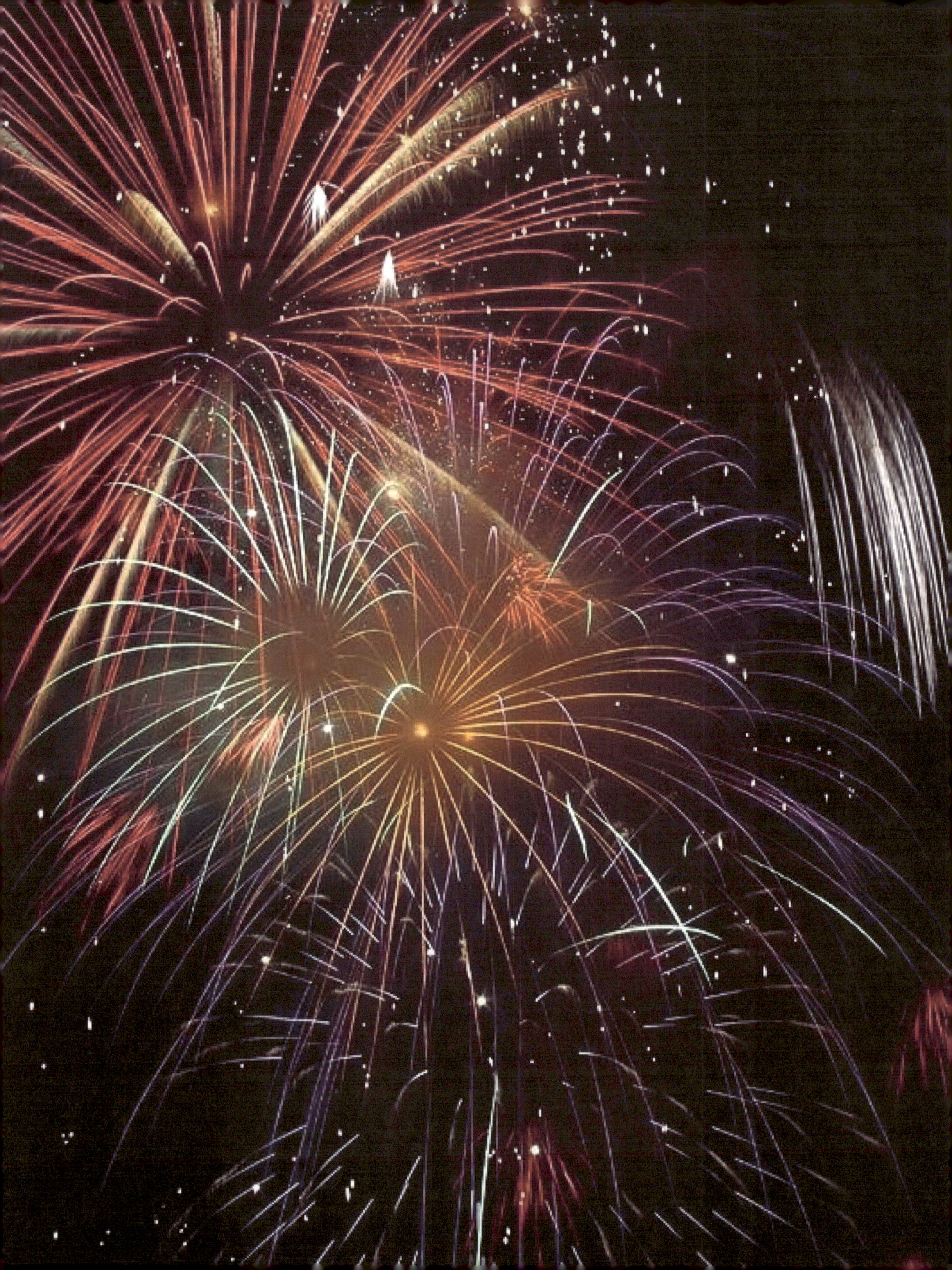

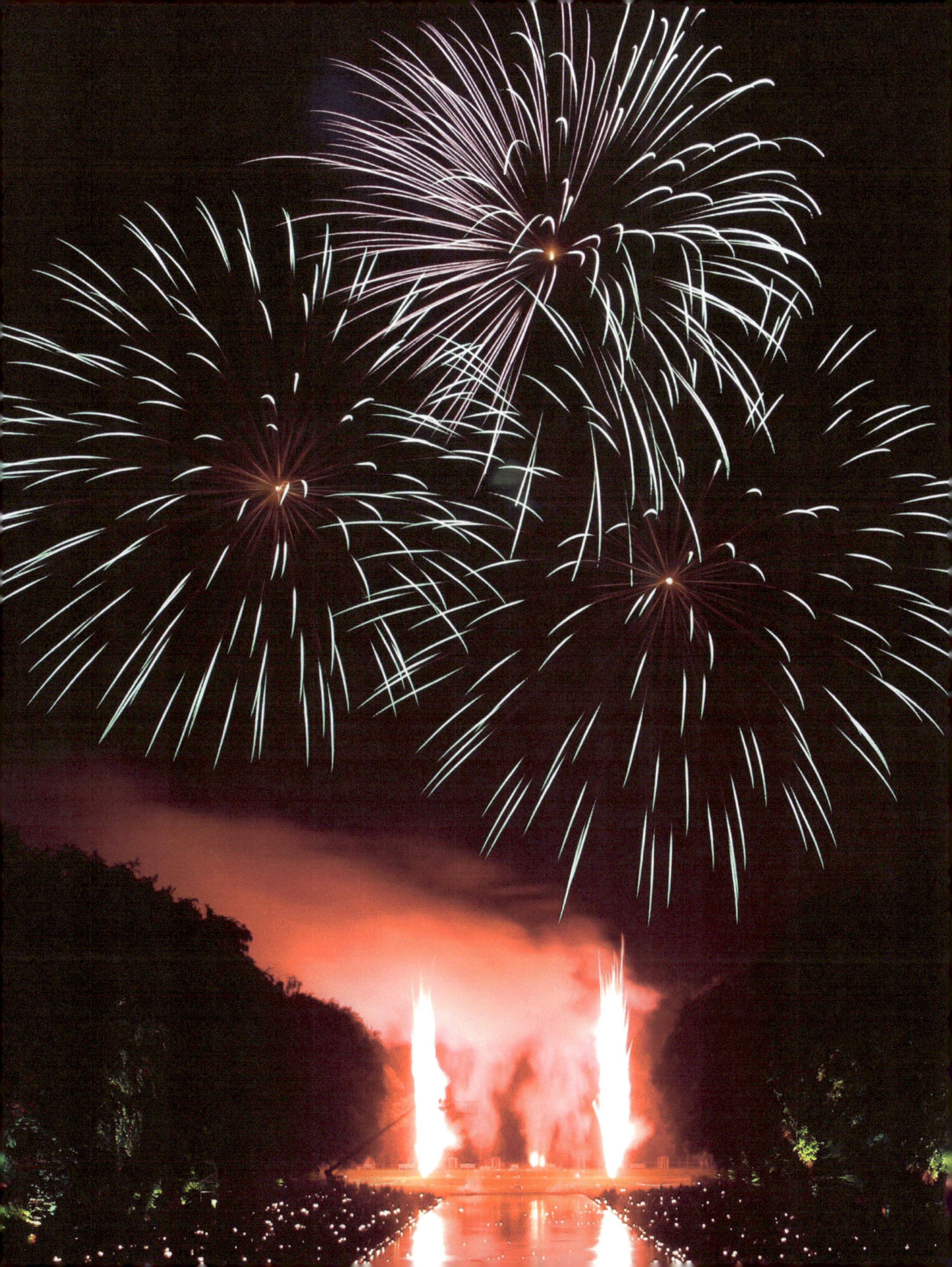

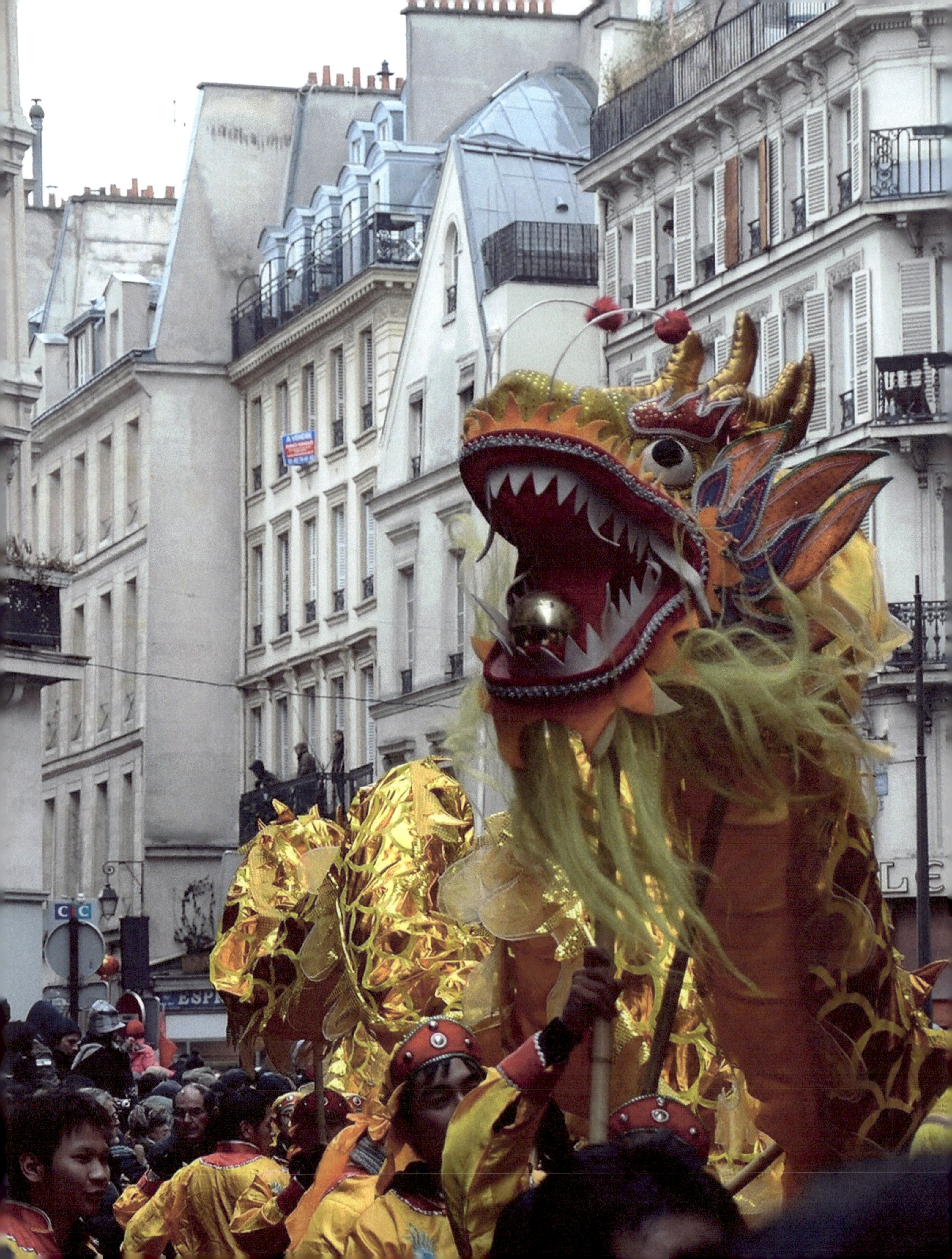

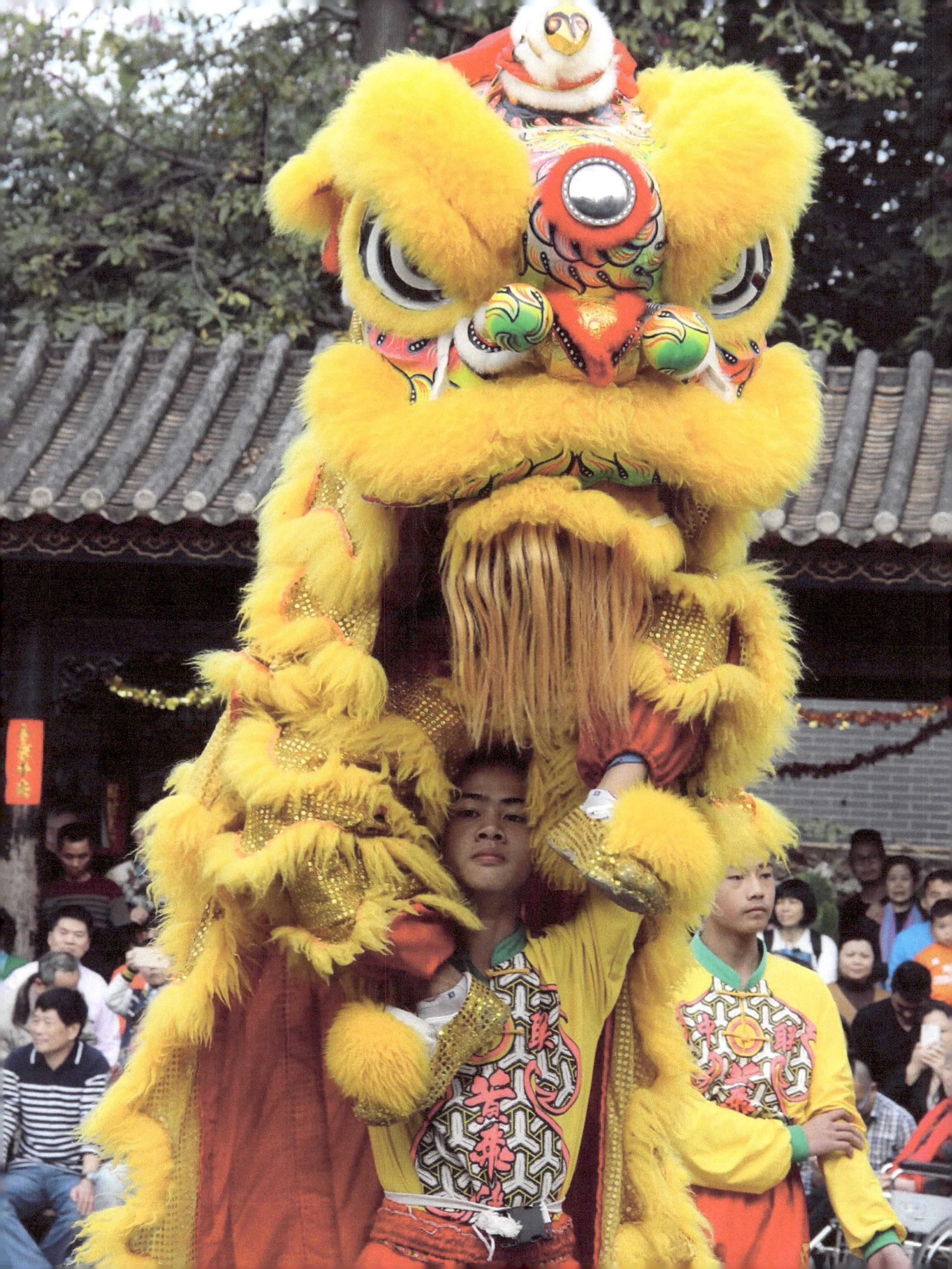

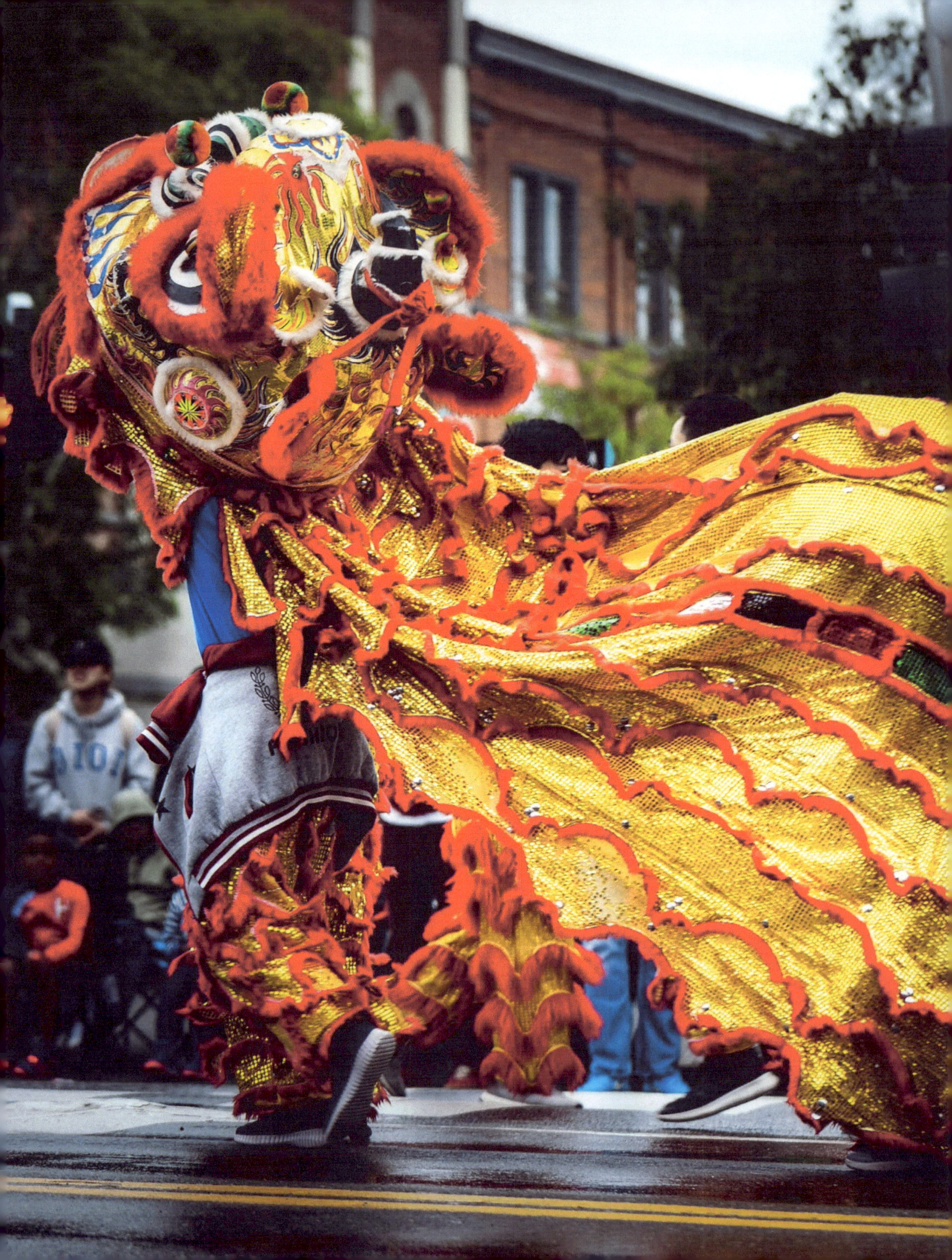

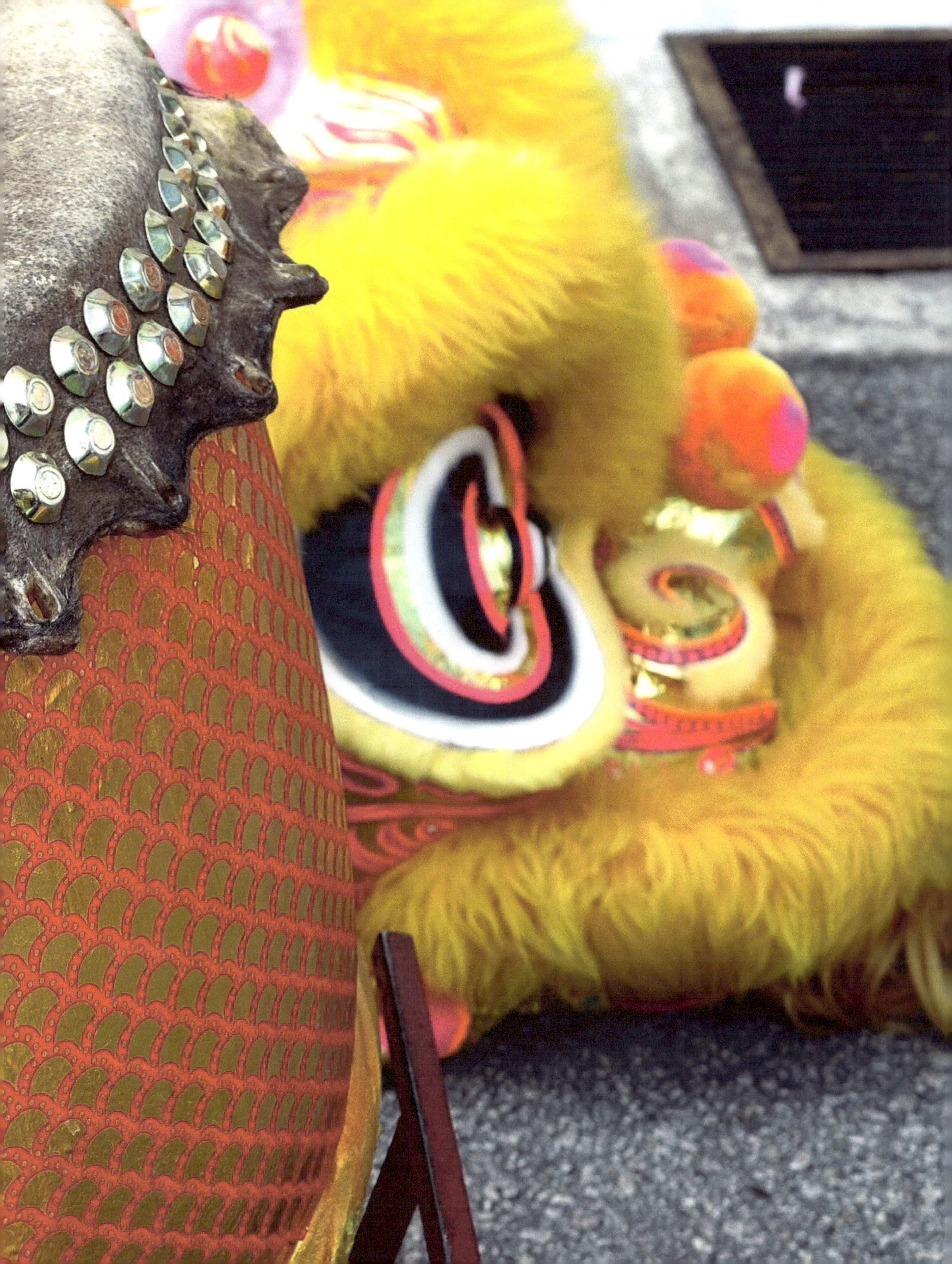

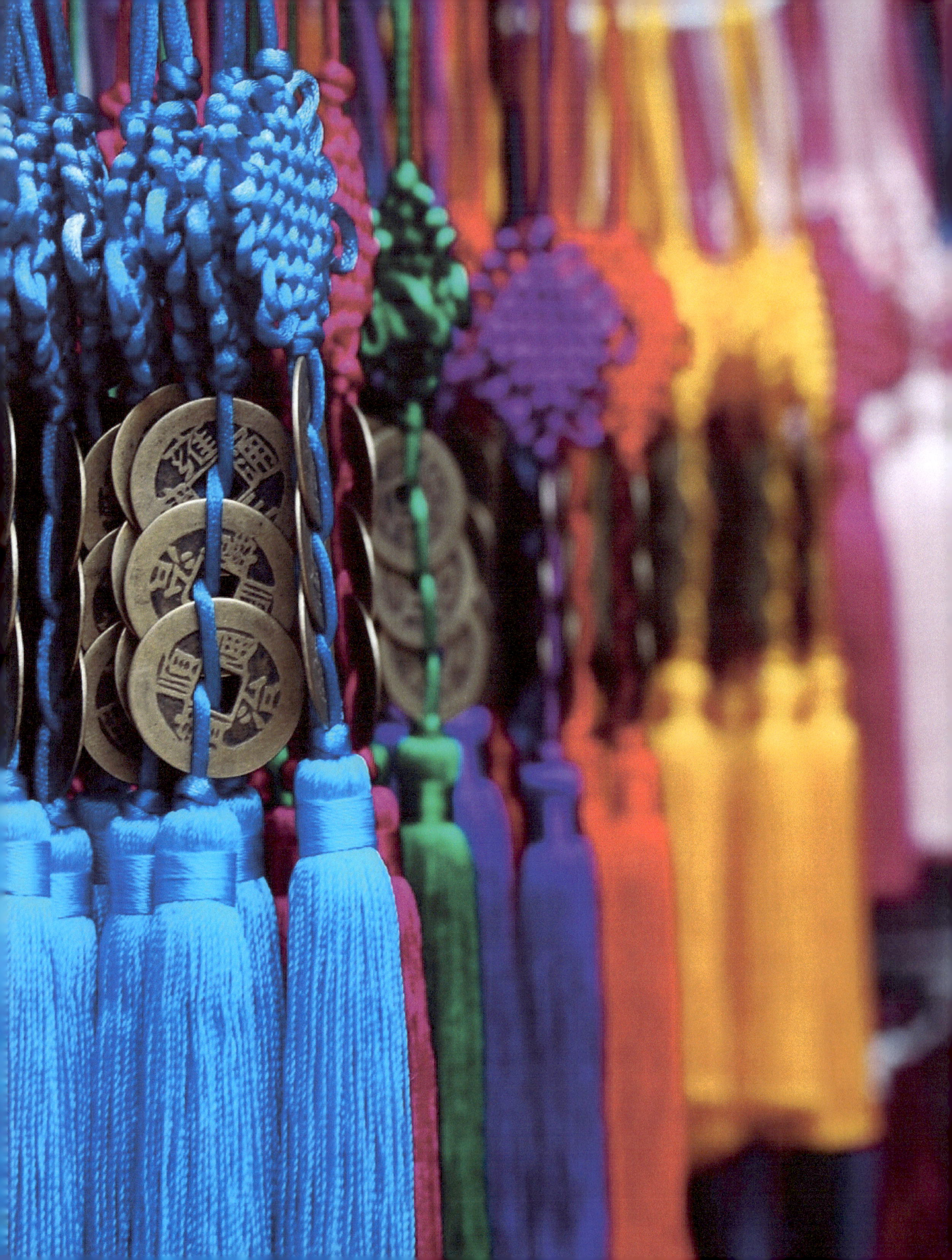

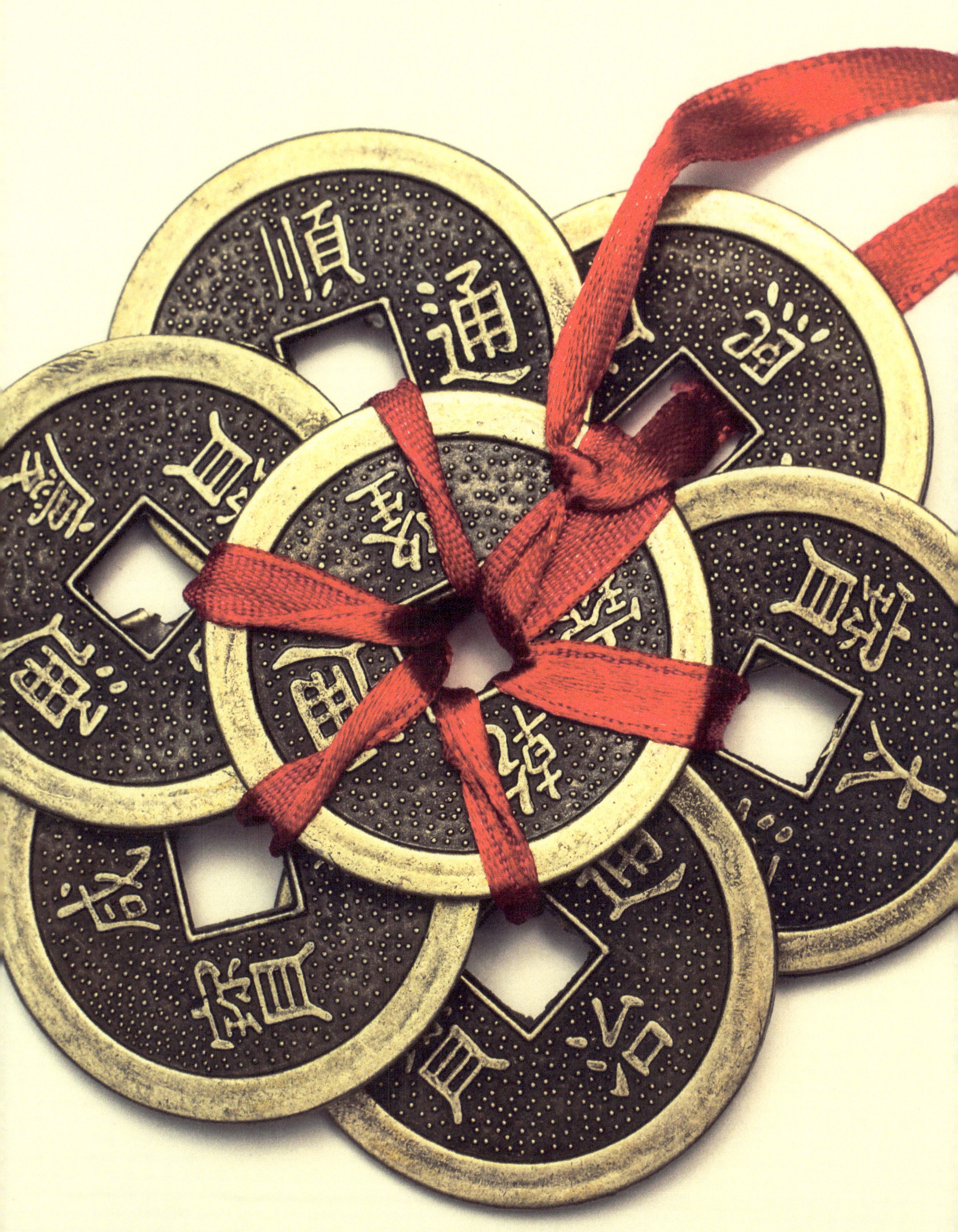

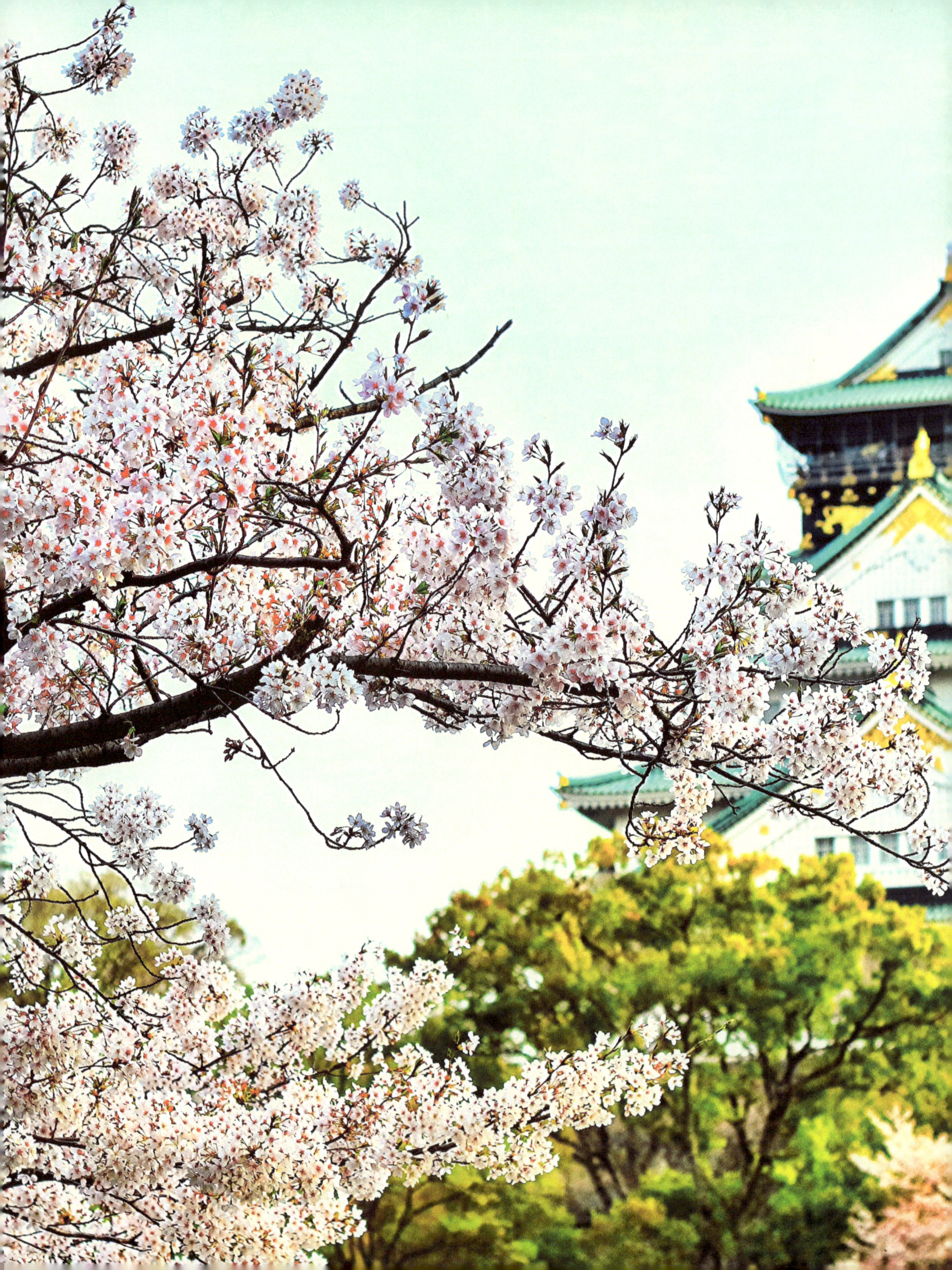

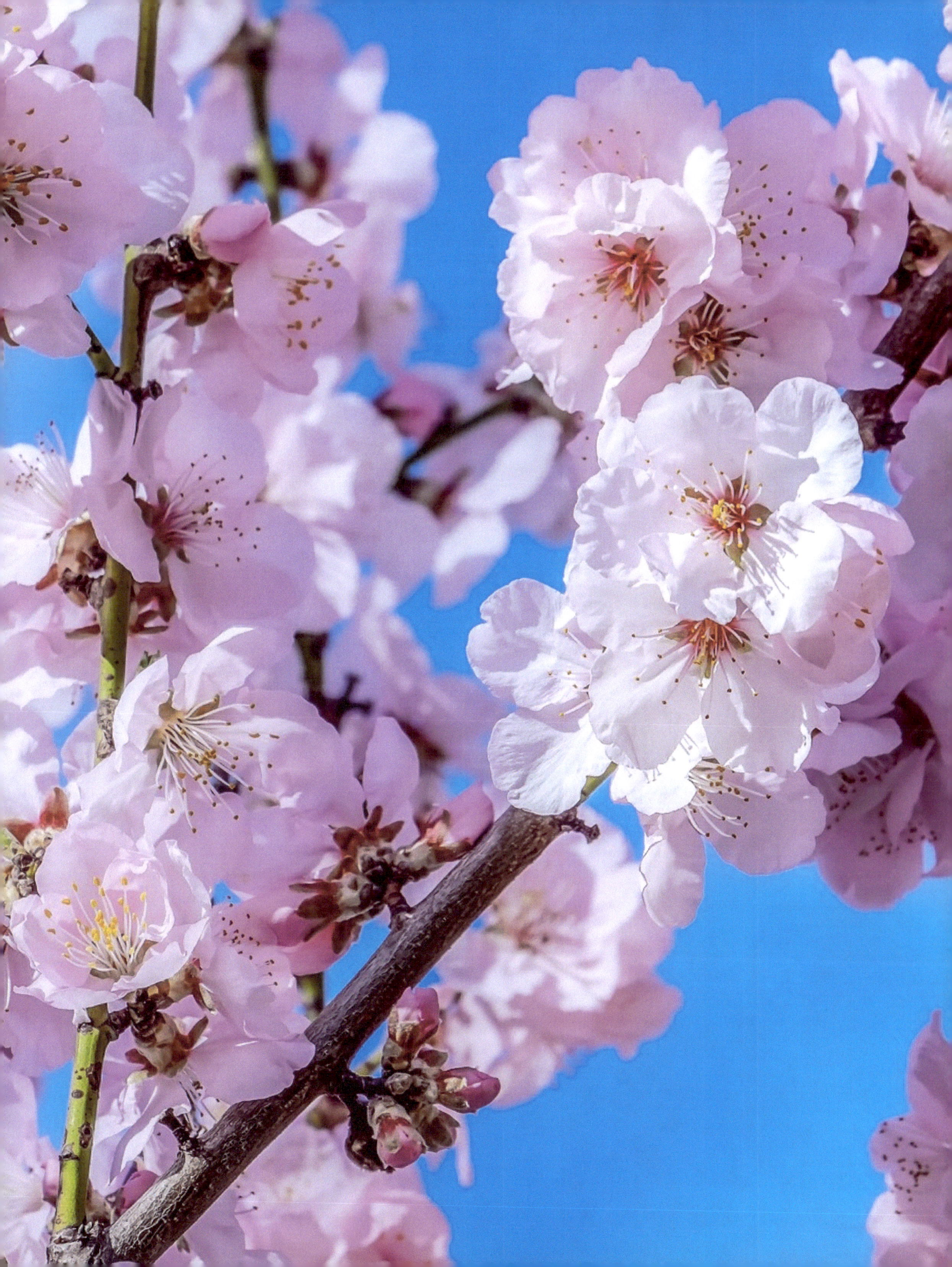

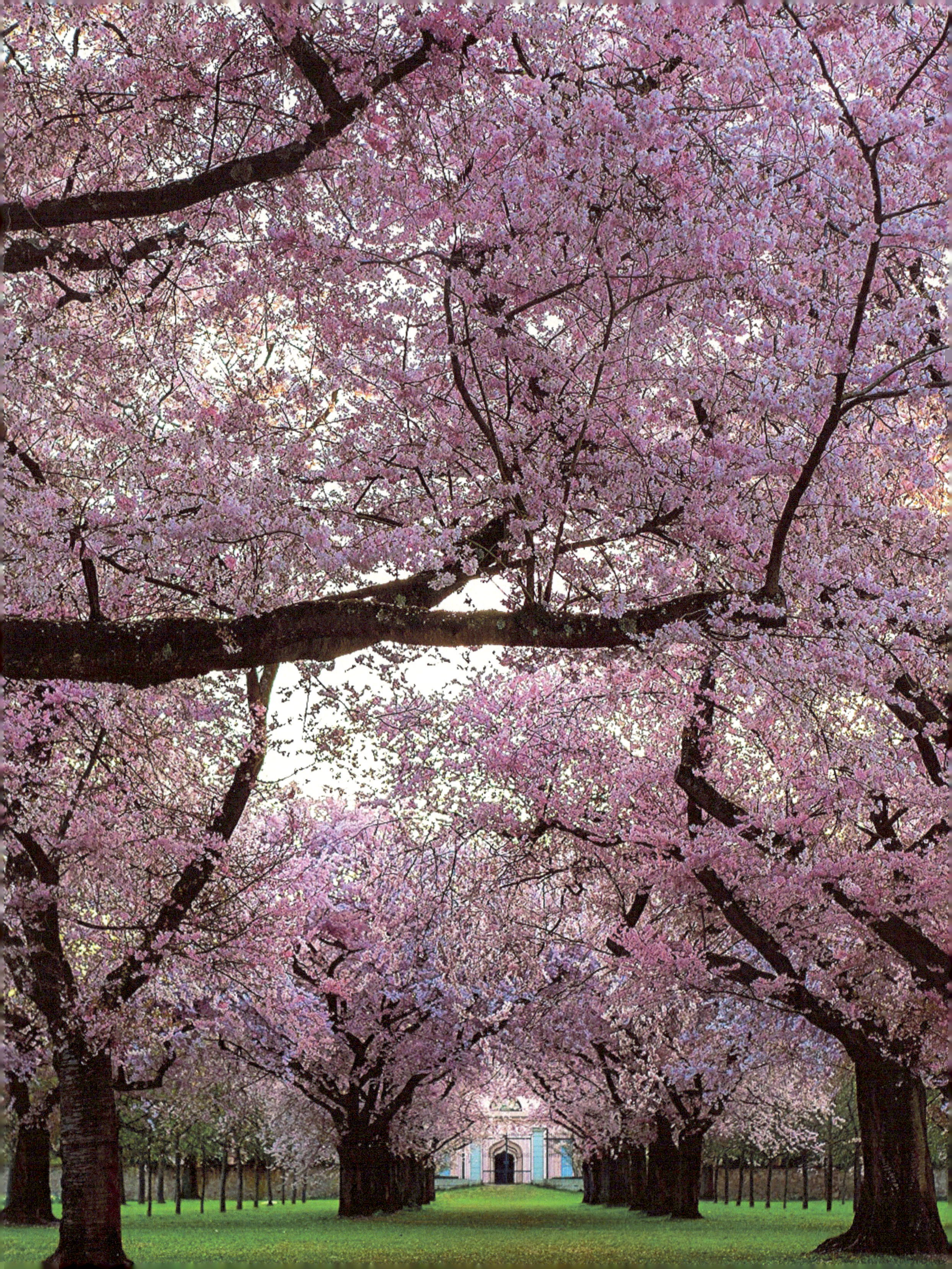

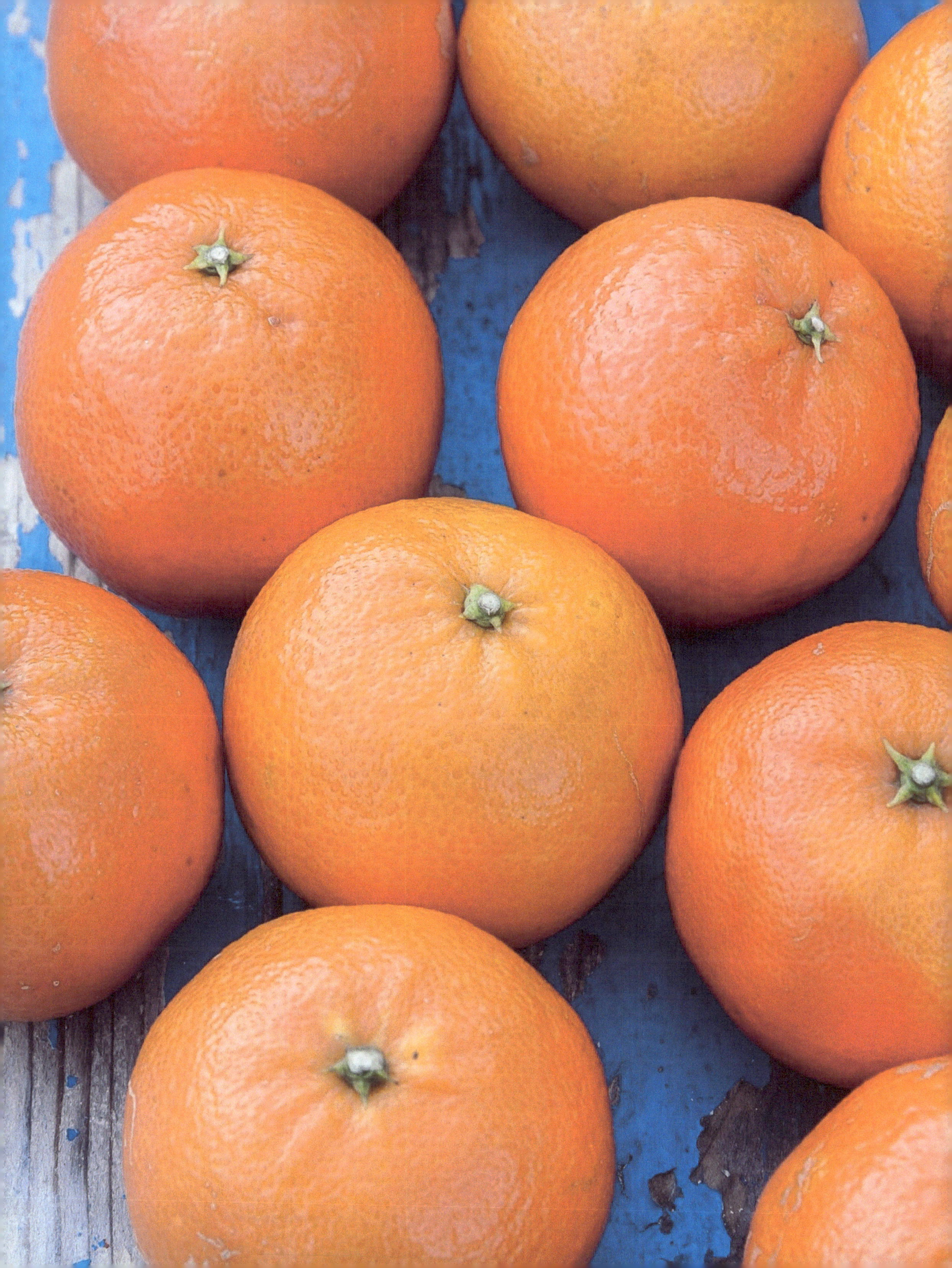

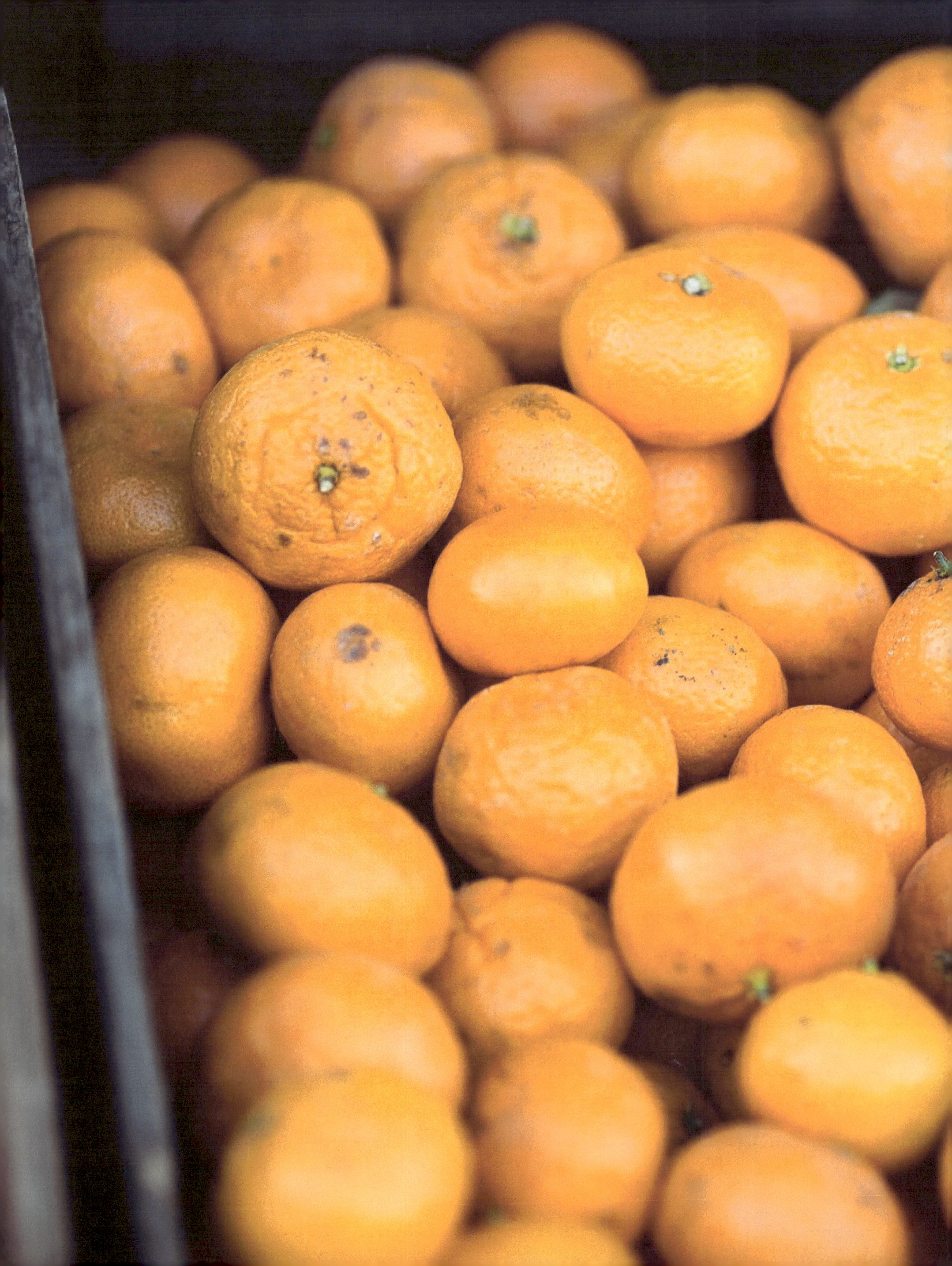

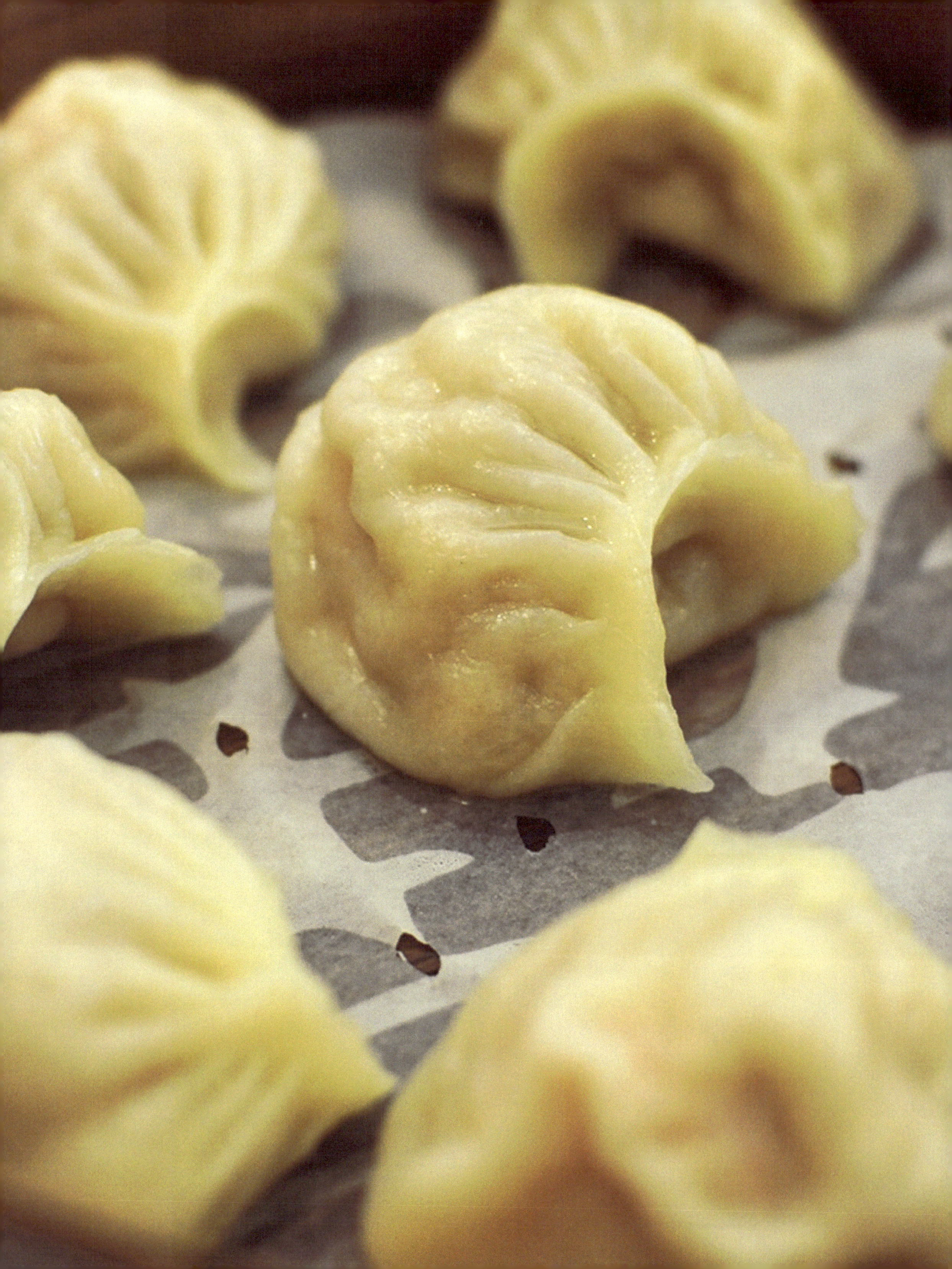

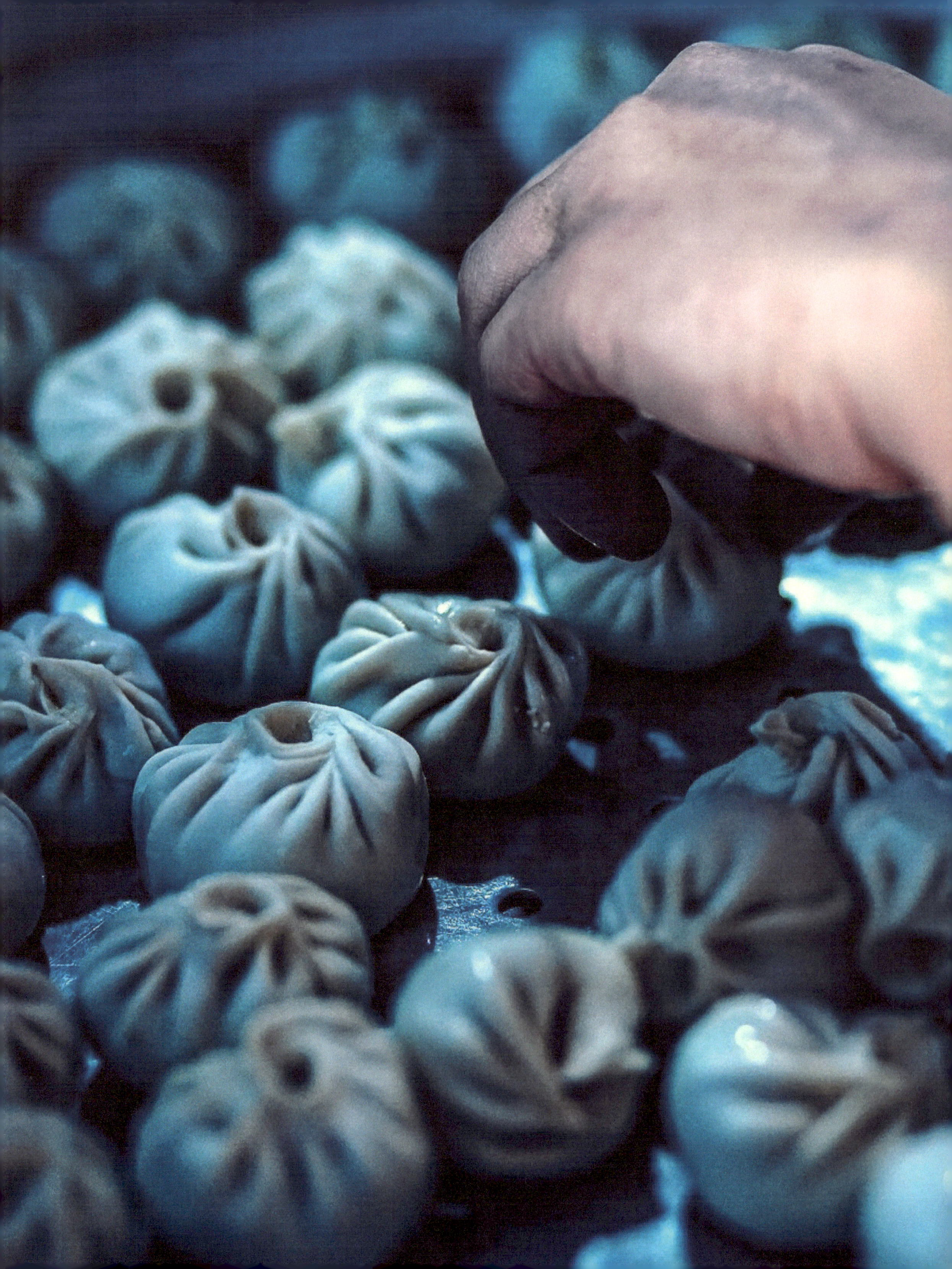

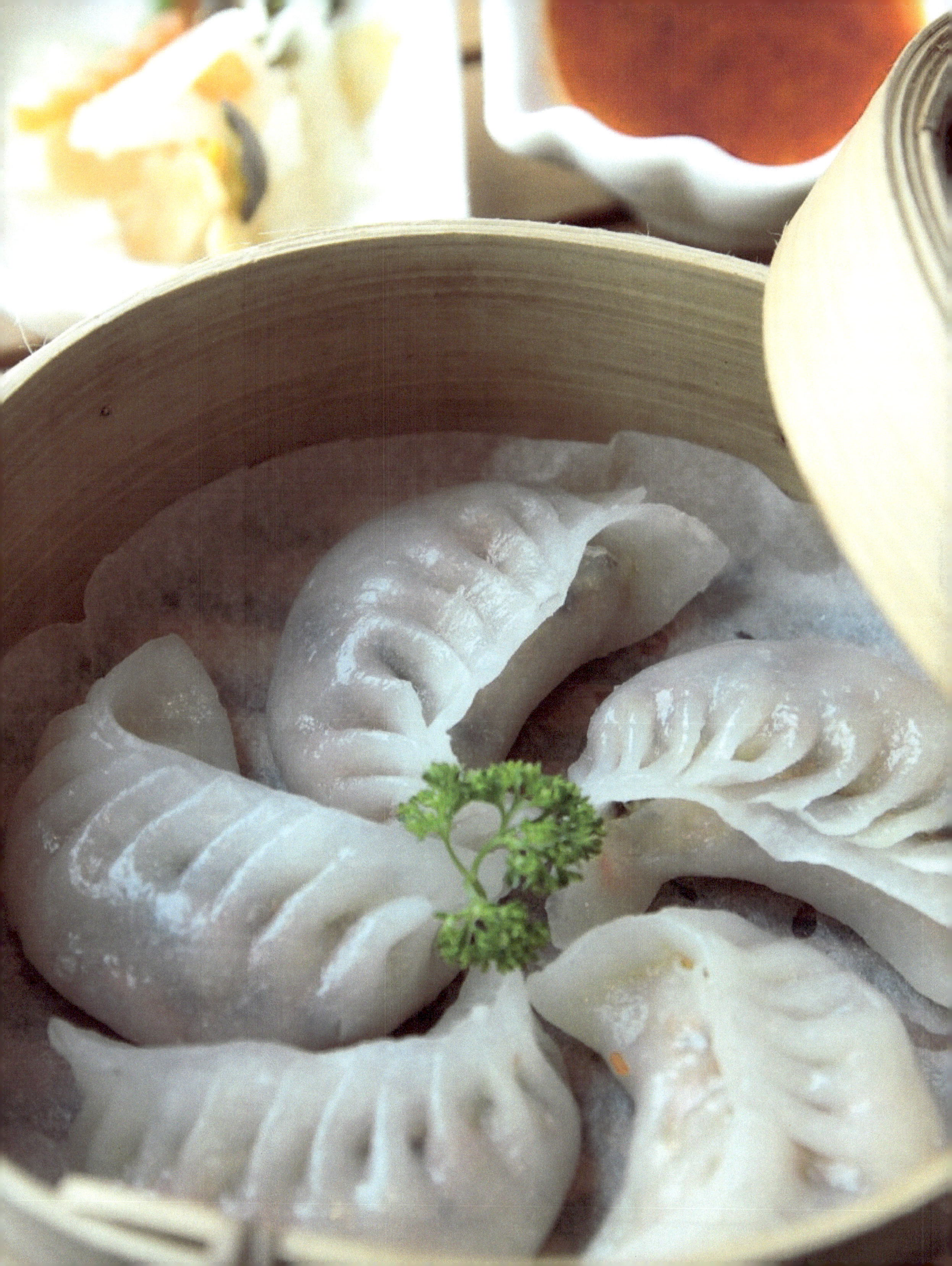

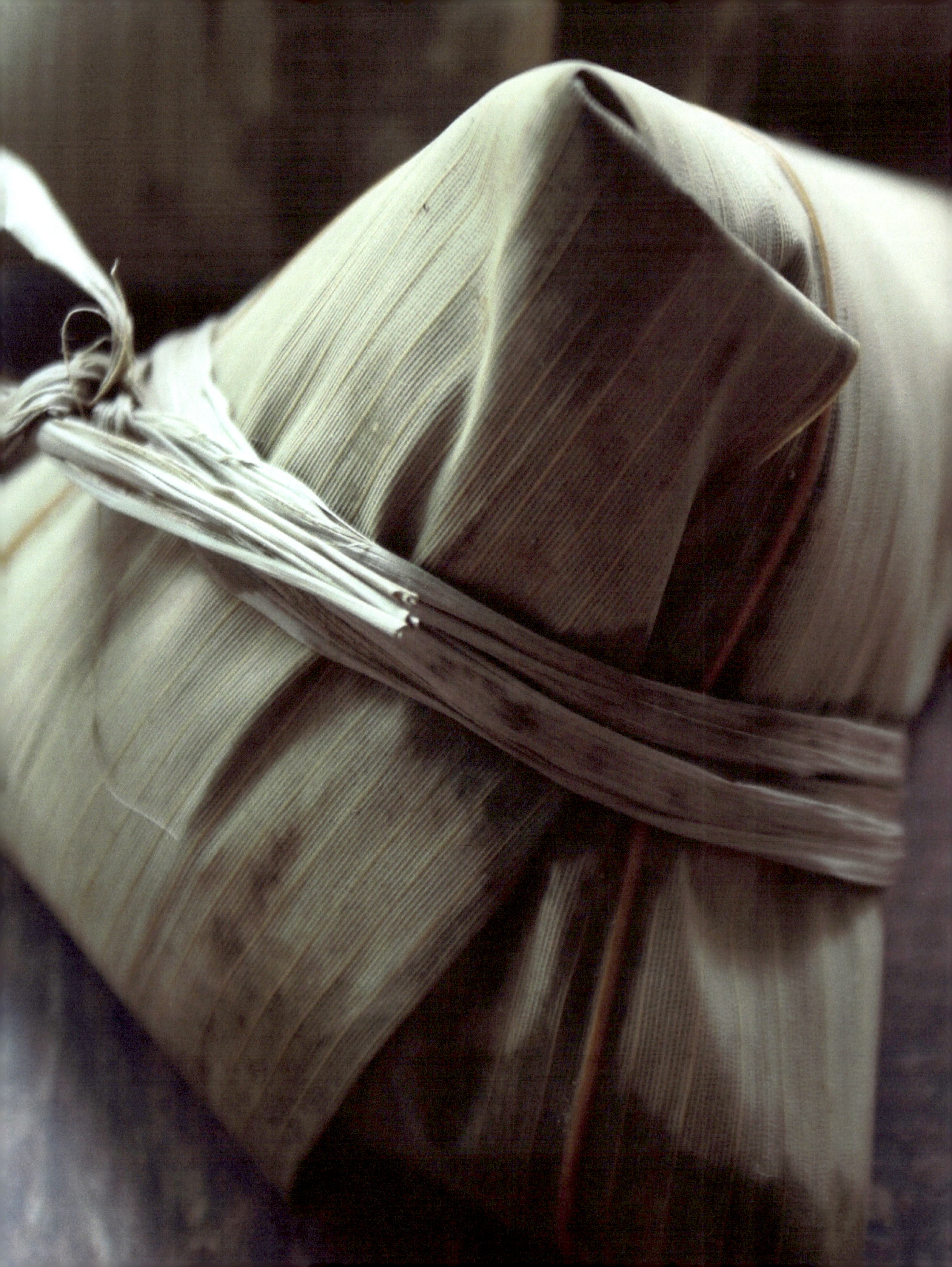

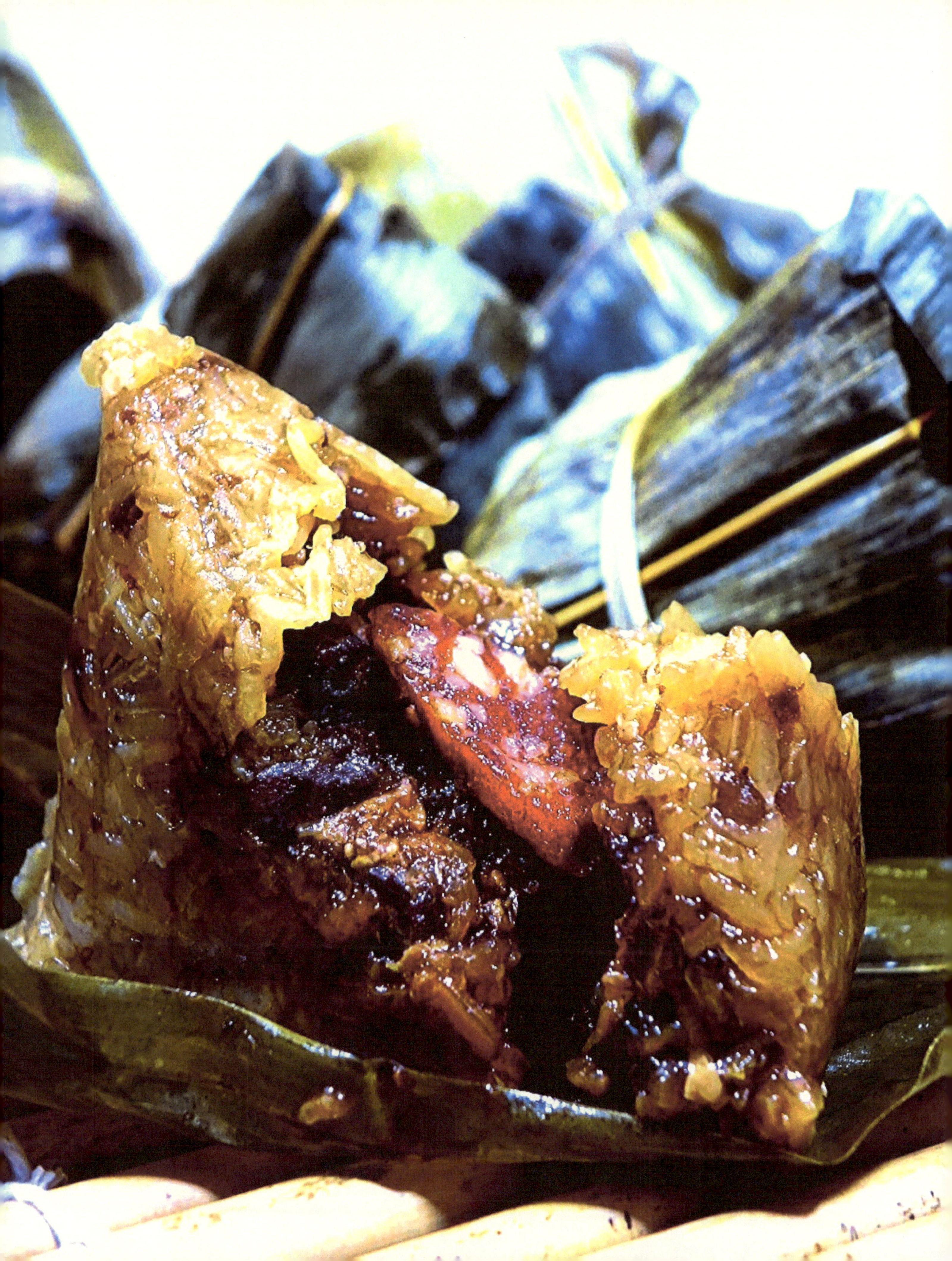

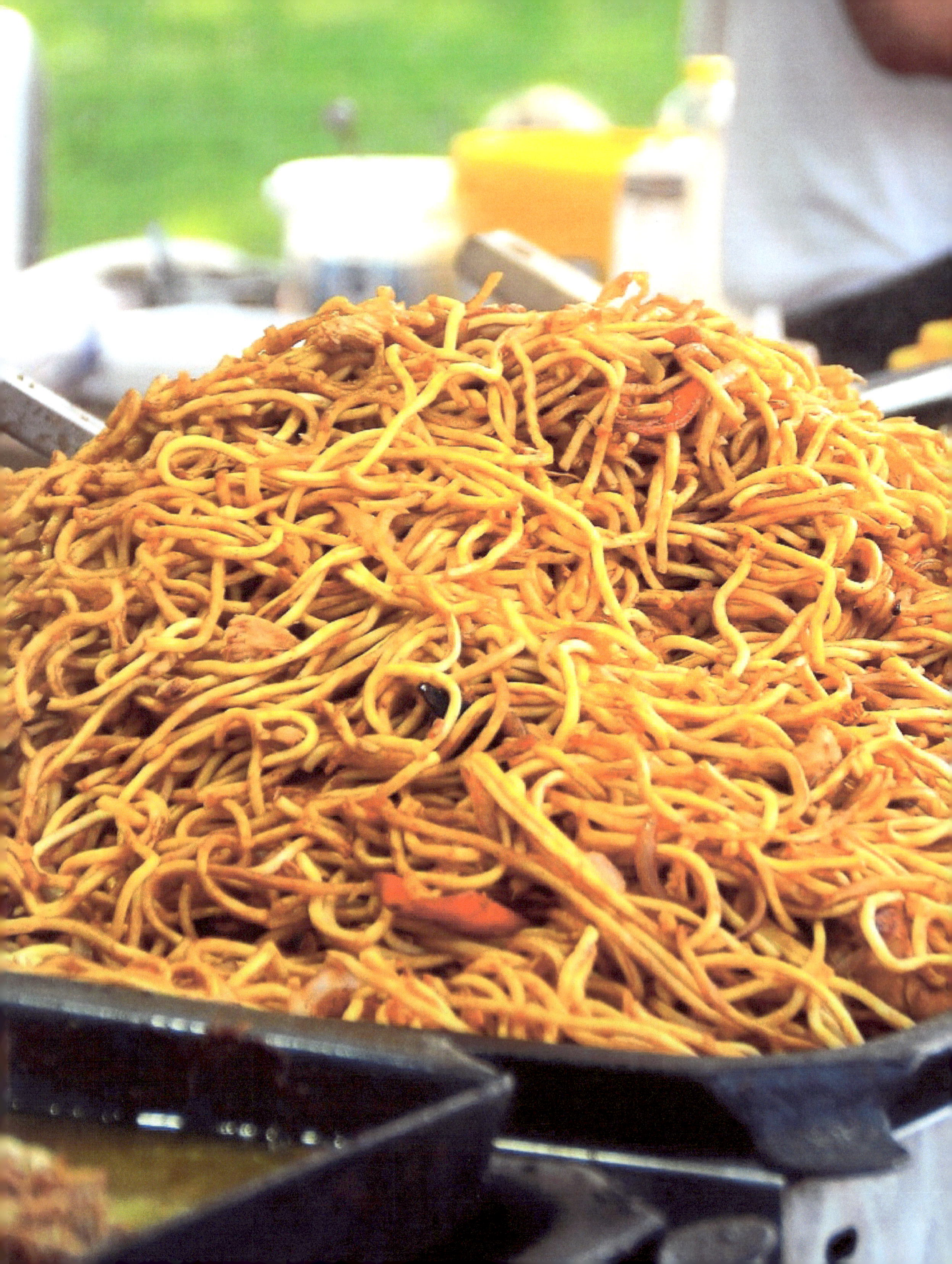

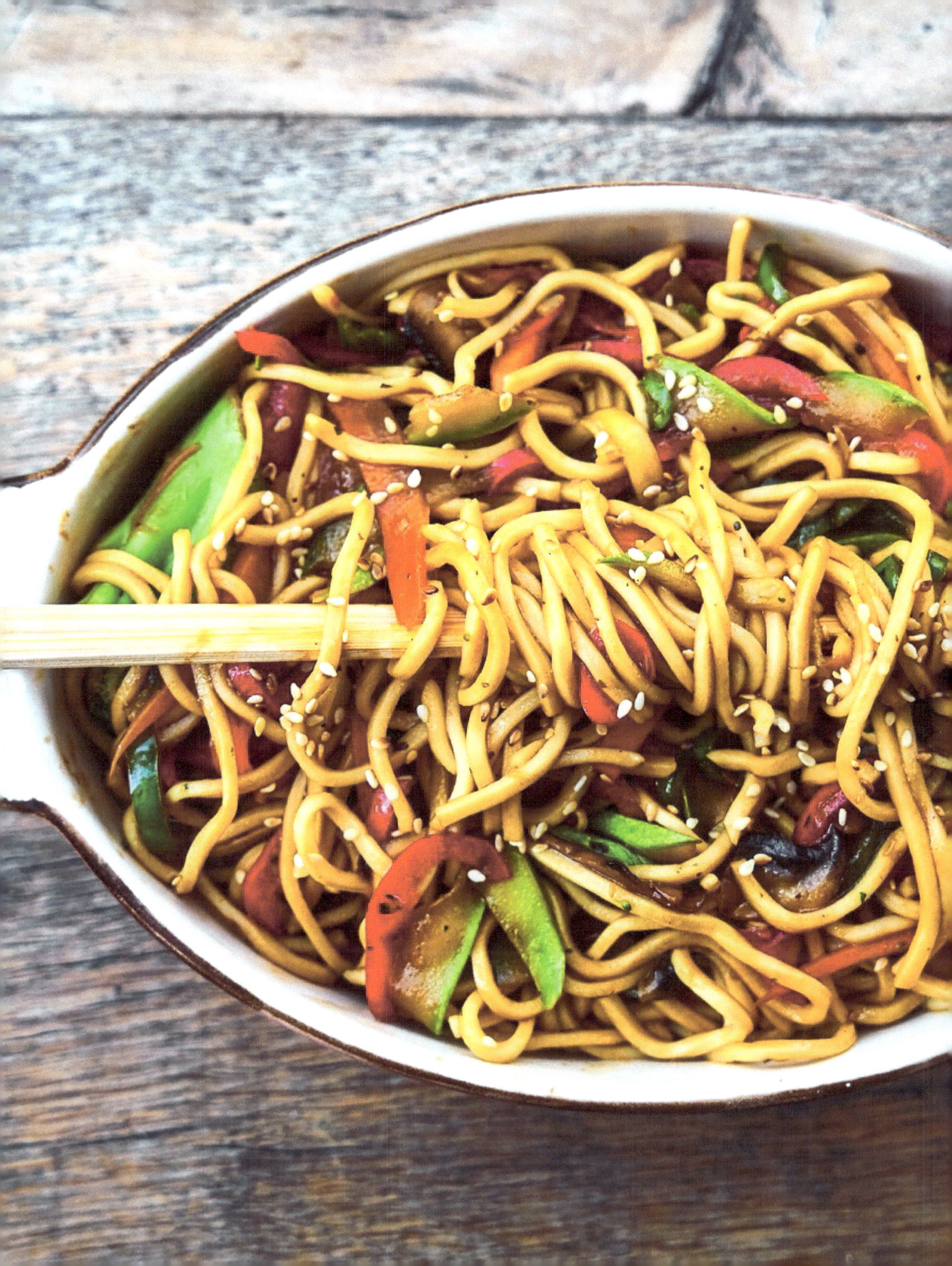

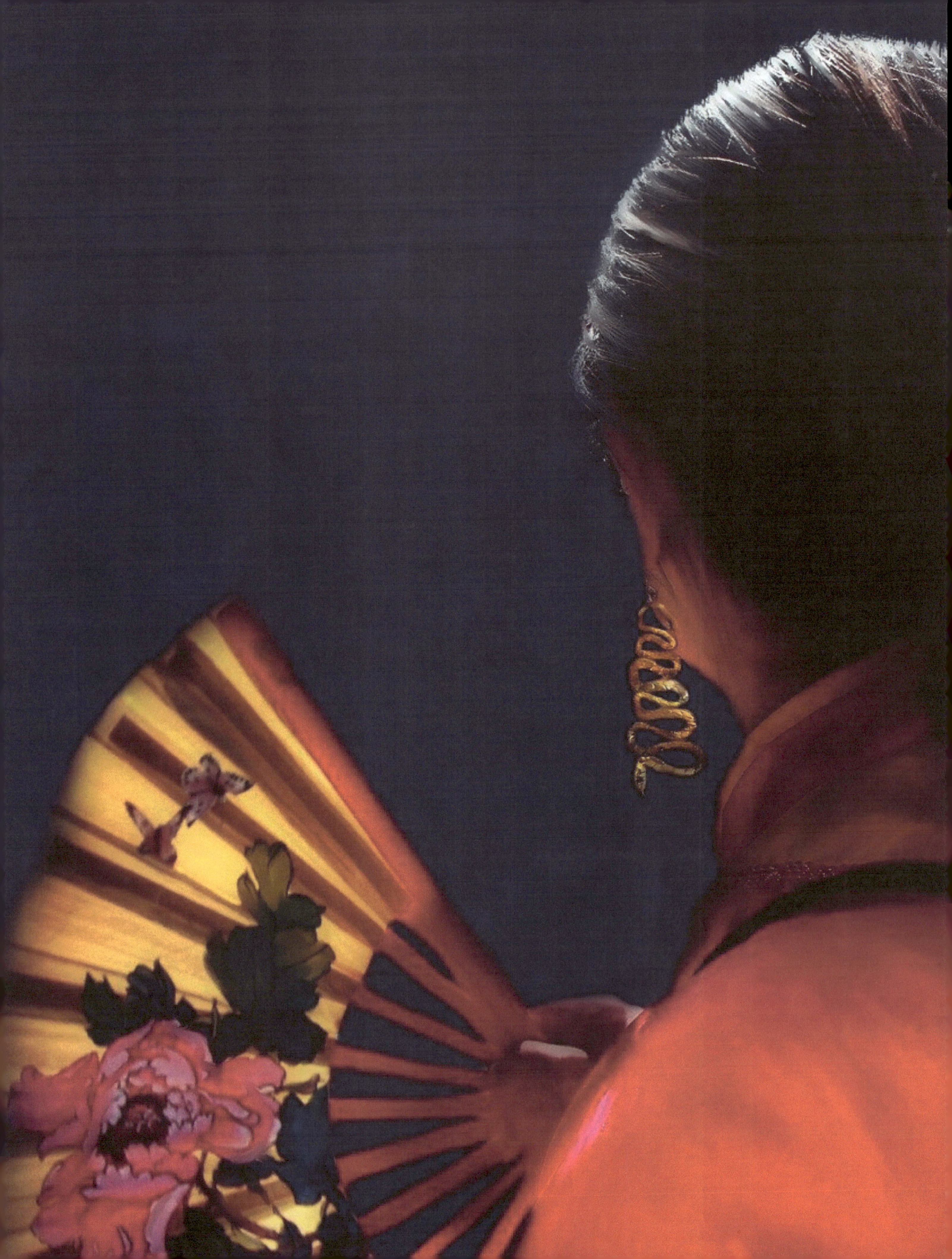

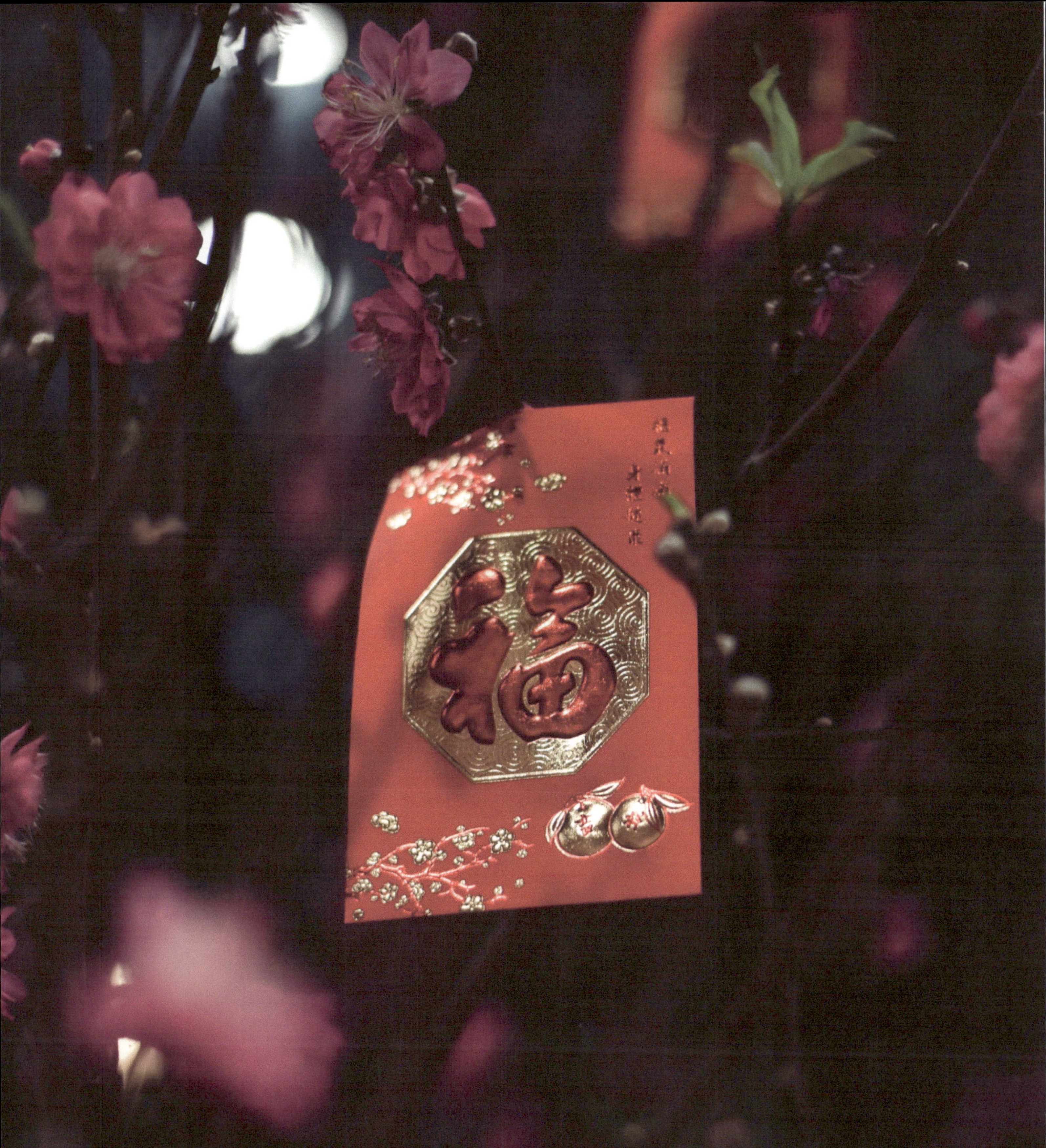

福

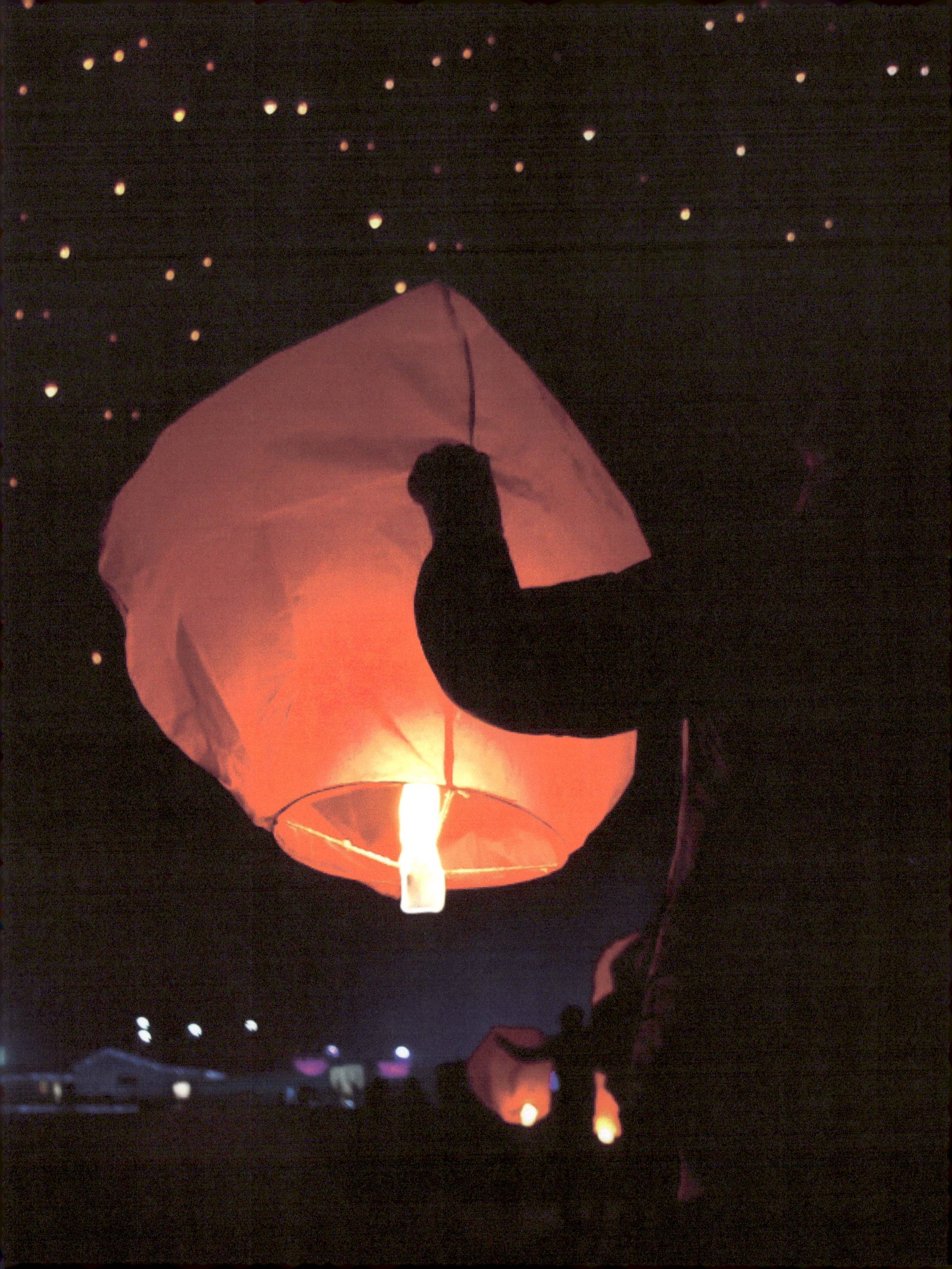

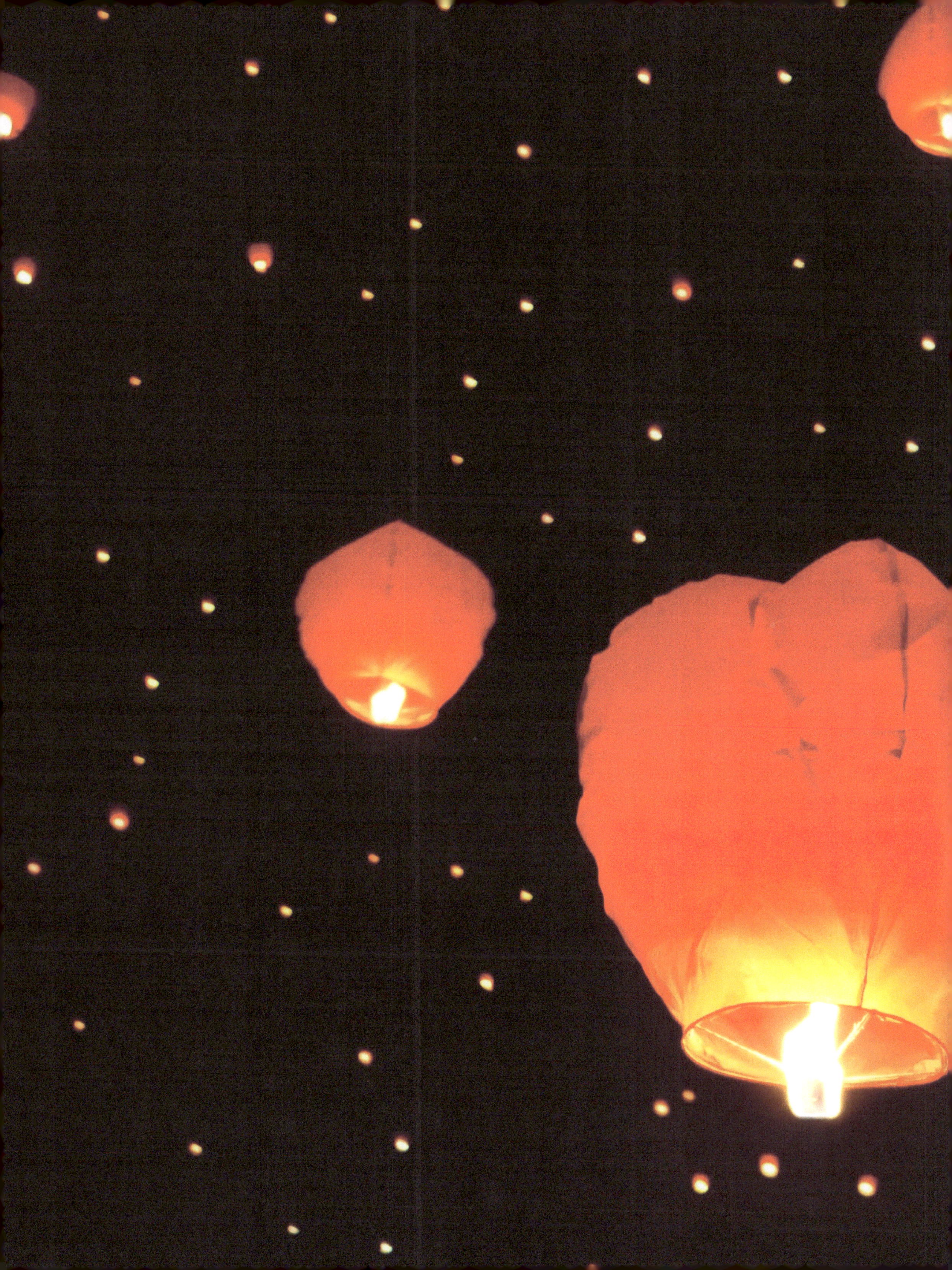

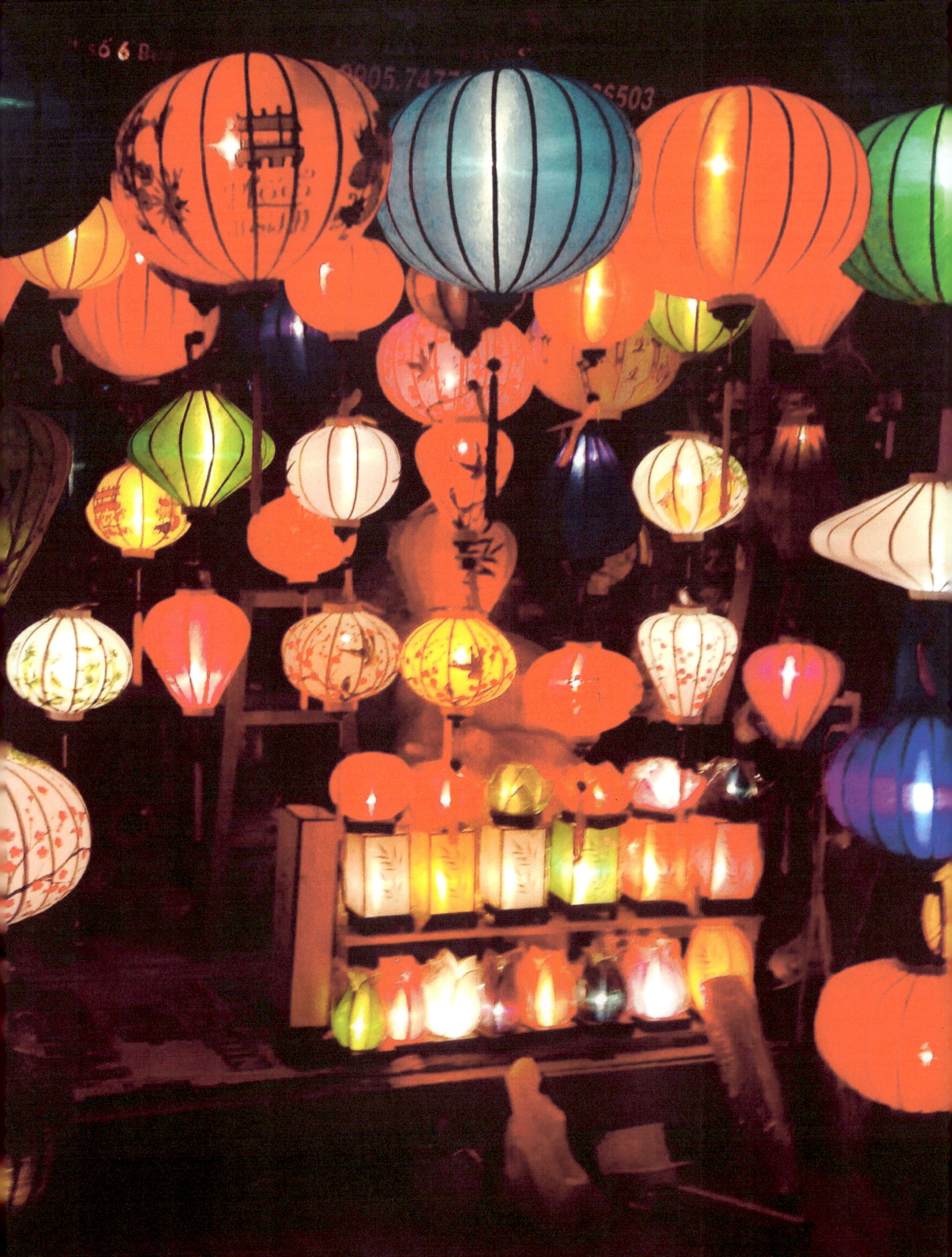
số 6 B
0905.747
66503

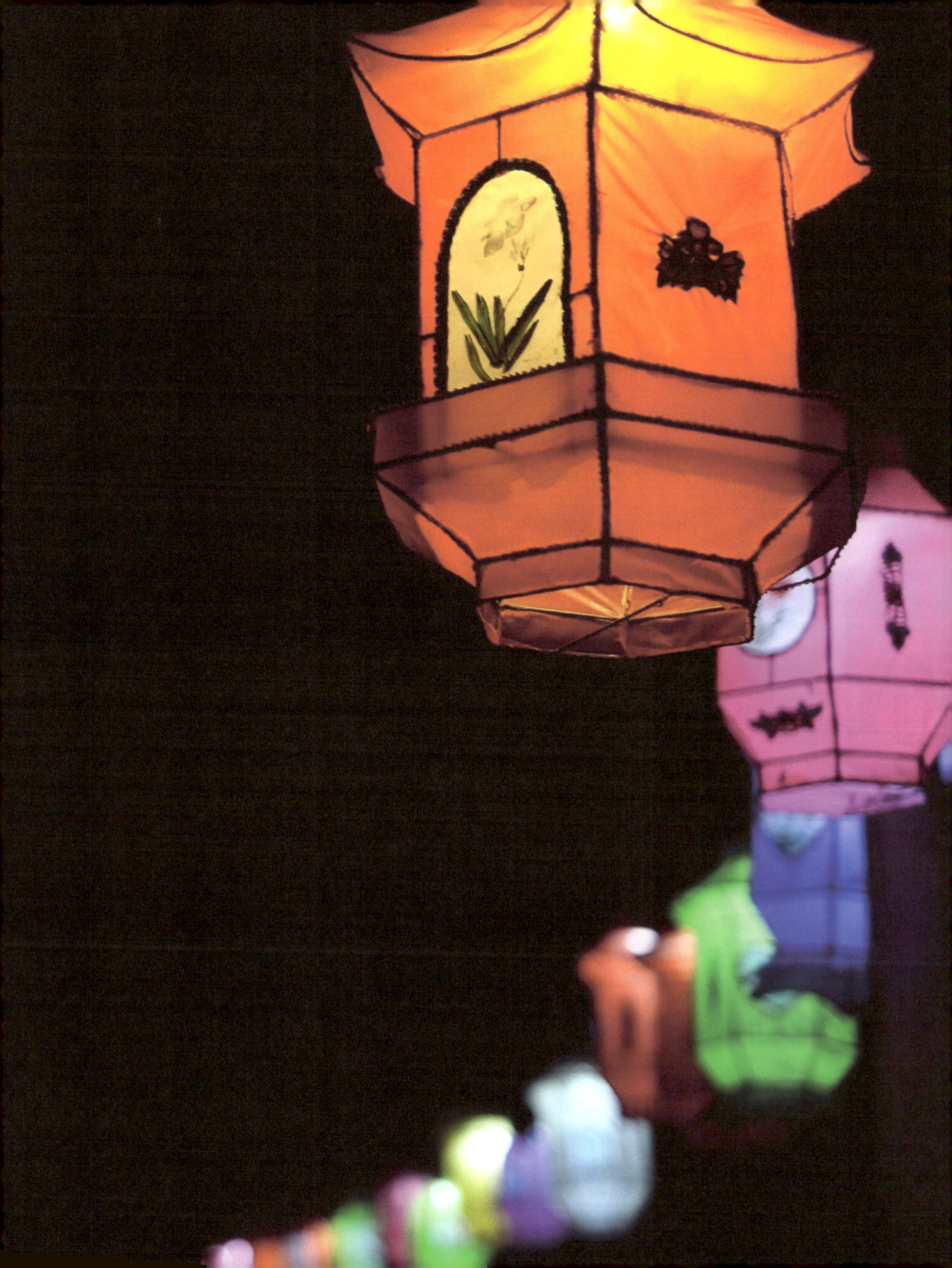

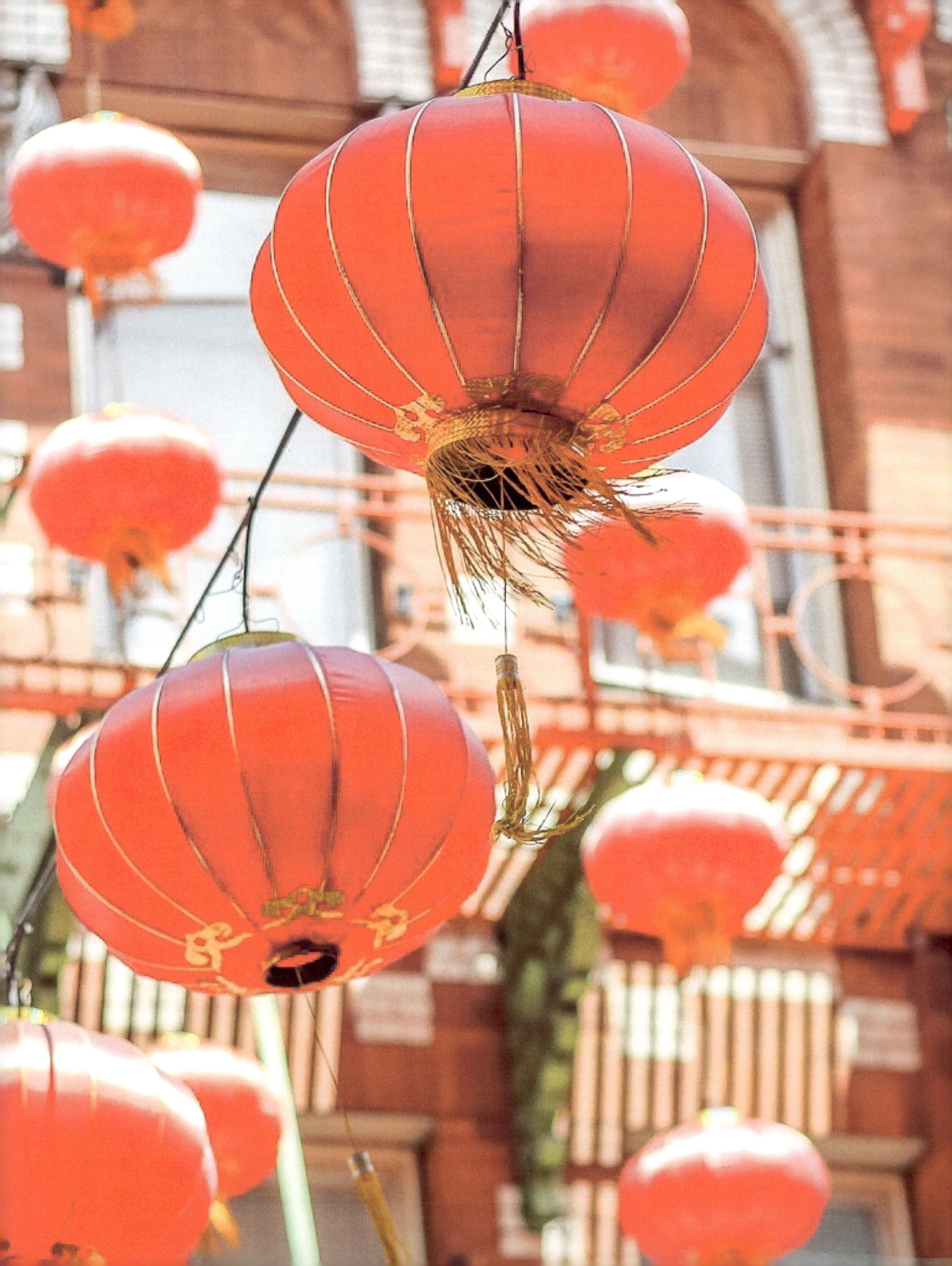

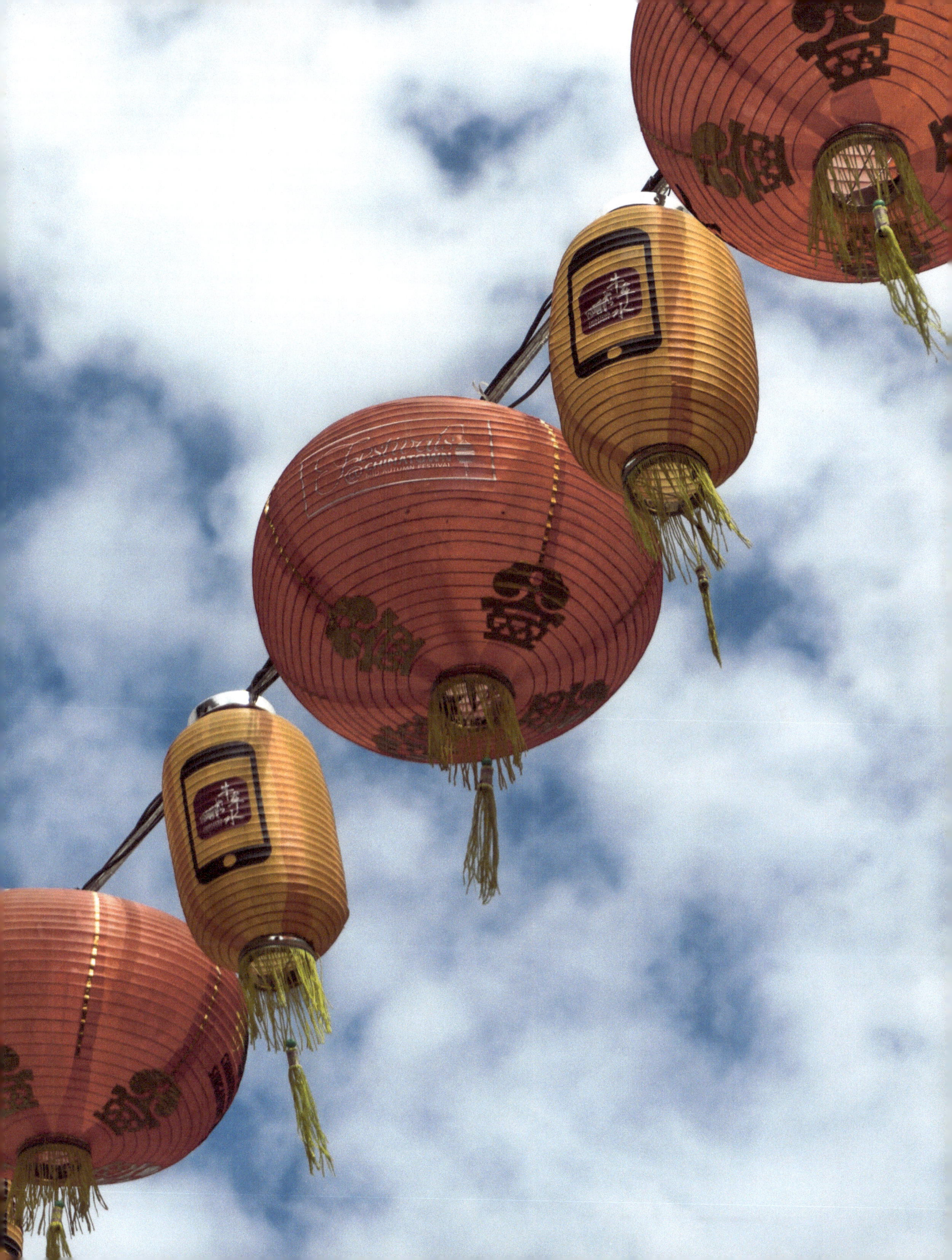

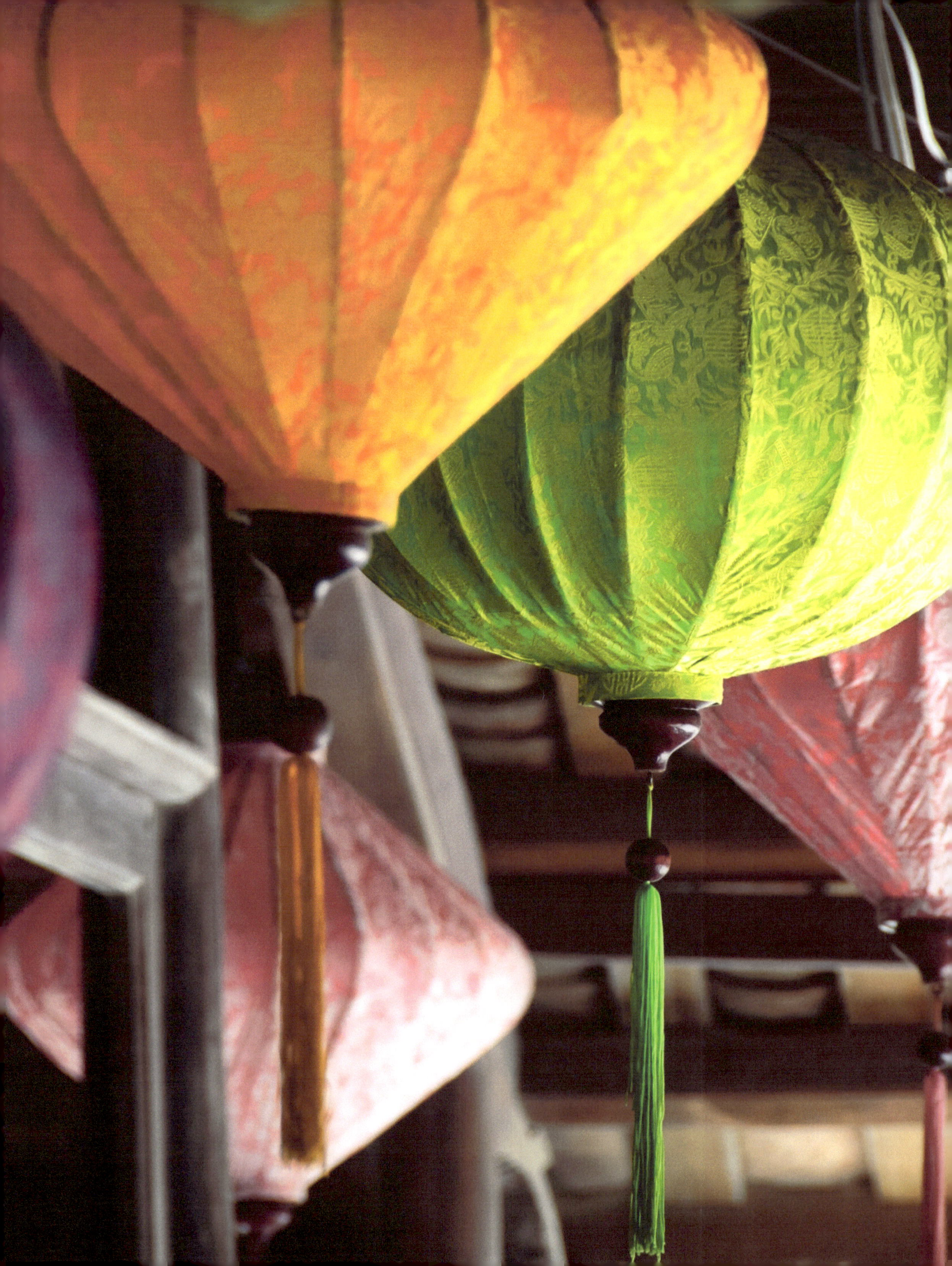

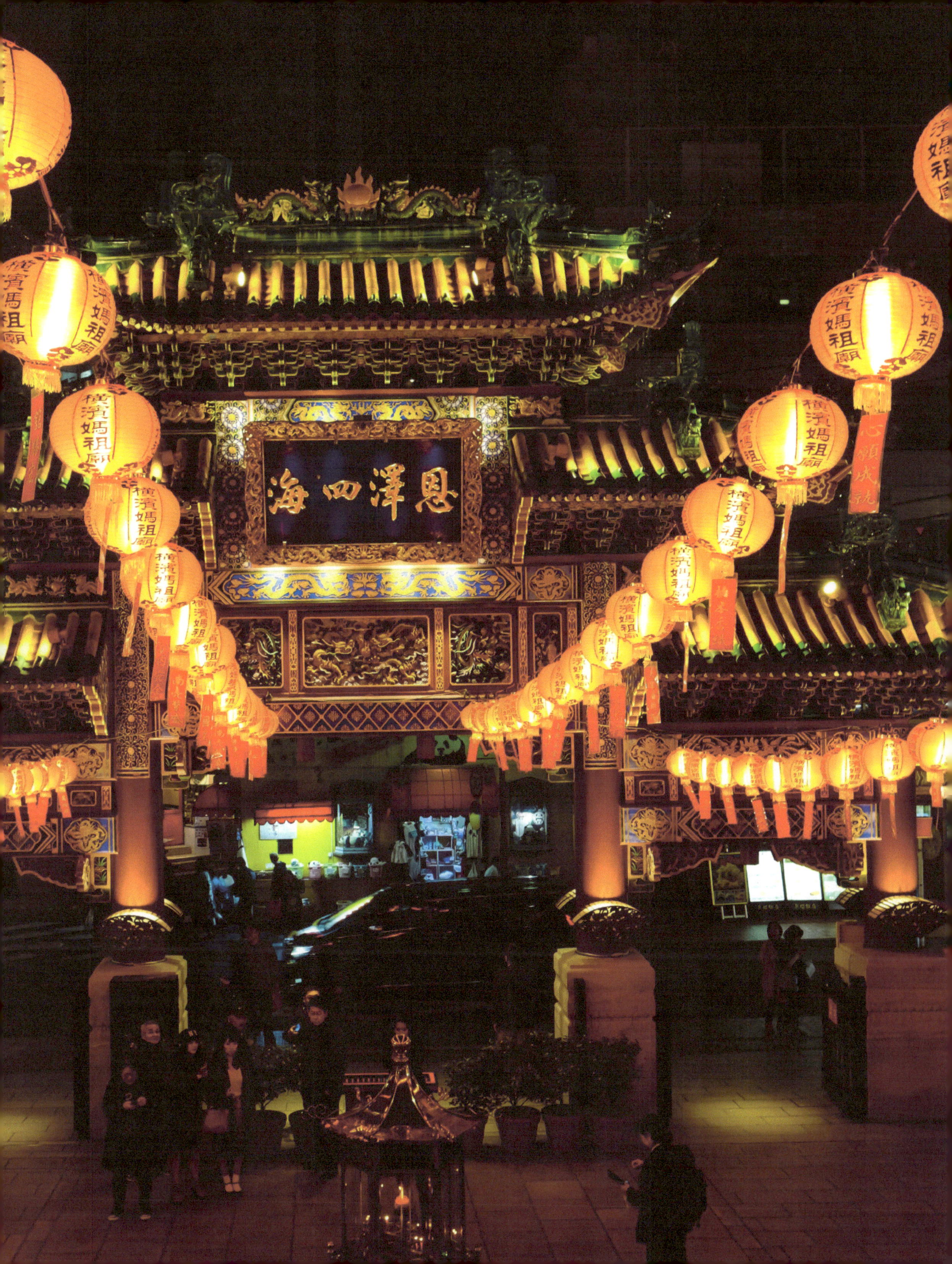

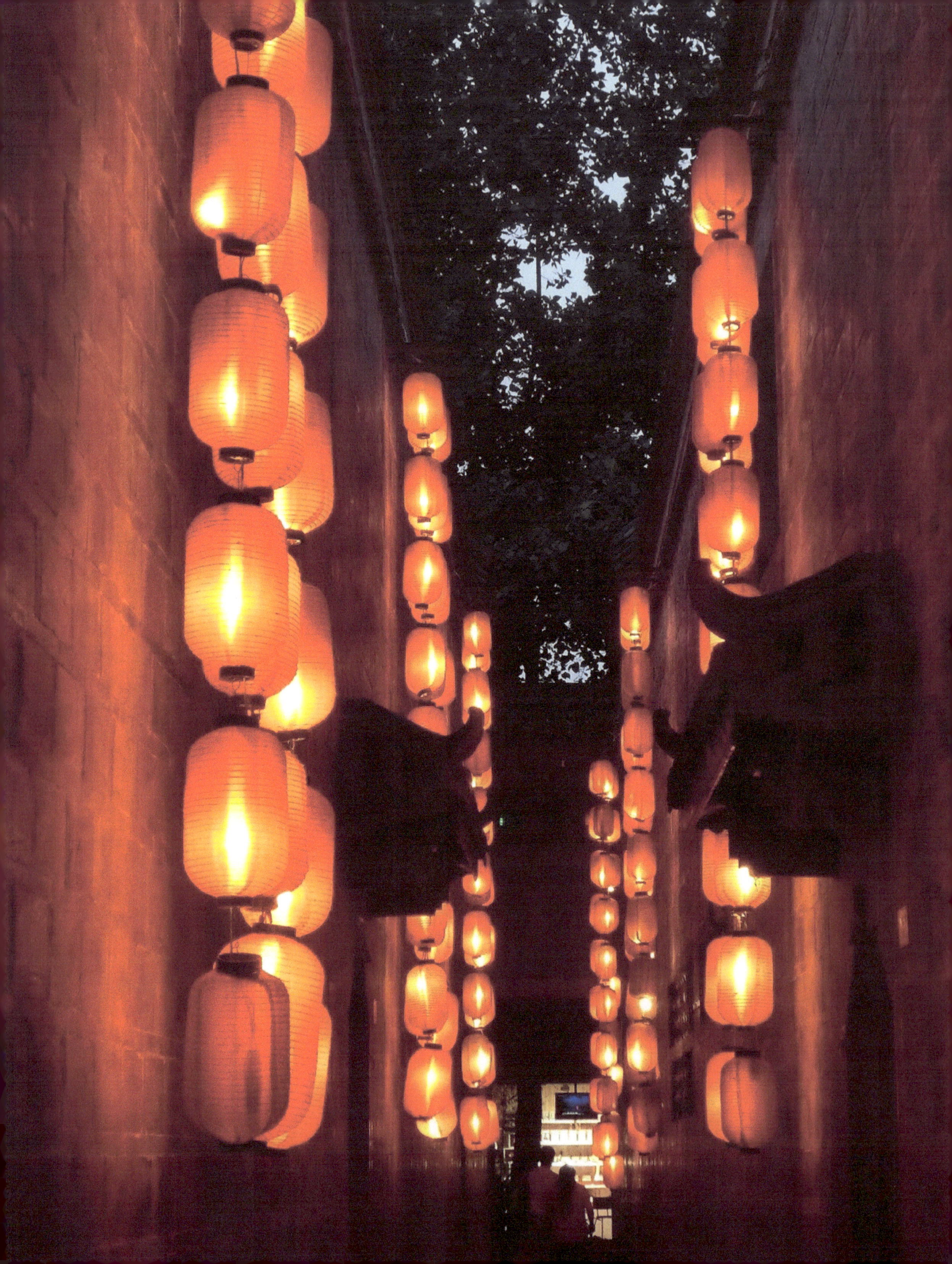

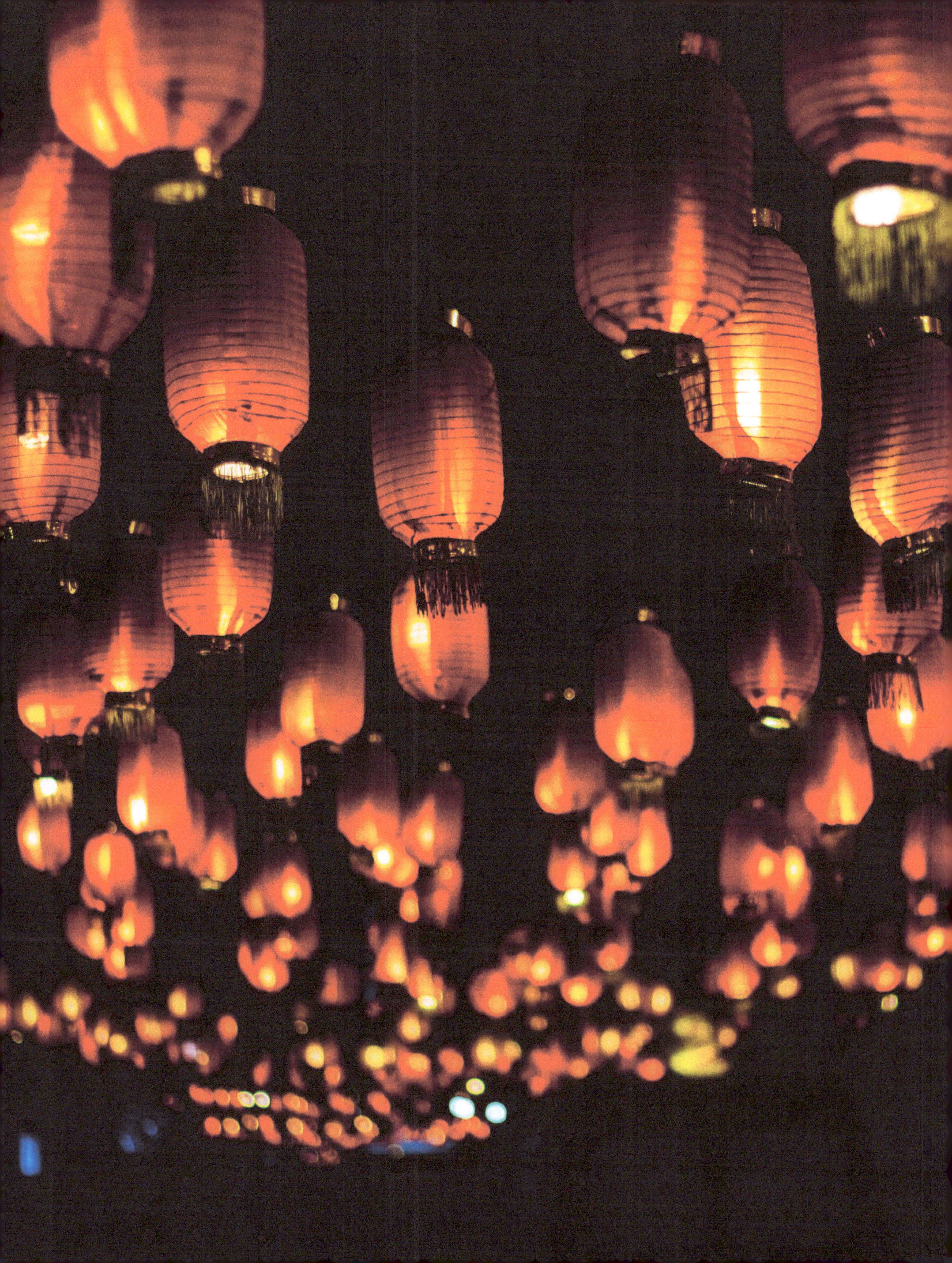

Xin Nian Kuai Le!
May Your Year Be Blessed with
Great Health
Abundant Fortune
and
Magnificent Happiness

Blitzen Road Books
Source of Photos: Canva, Pexels, Pixabay, and Unsplash